W9-BKD-319

Advisor Today's

Sizzling
Sales Ideas

Compiled by the Editors of *Advisor Today*

Advisor Today's Sizzling Sales Ideas
Copyright ©2004 by NAIFA. All rights reserved.
Printed in the United States of America.

All inquiries should be addressed to:

NAIFA ₛₘ

A publication of the National Association
of Insurance and Financial Advisors

2901 Telestar Court, Falls Church, Virginia 22042

ISBN: 0-9741613-0-6

TABLE OF CONTENTS

INTRODUCTION

Persuading people to do what is right for the future at the cost of doing without some of the luxuries to which they have grown accustomed is no small feat. But this is what financial advisors do each day as they persuade and cajole family members, friends, acquaintances and strangers to spend time and money developing plans that will provide the financial resources they need to protect their families and ensure a comfortable retirement.

To help you with this rewarding but challenging task, the editors of *Advisor Today* have compiled the best sales ideas from the magazine and proven strategies from the industry's top producers. The result is *Advisor Today's Sizzling Sales Ideas*, a practical guide to help you maximize your sales efforts and enhance your practice.

Whether you are new to the business or a seasoned pro, *Sizzling Sales Ideas* will give you the tips and tools you need to excel at the fine art of selling financial products and services. It is jam-packed with time-tested techniques from industry veterans, new takes on old problems and cost-efficient approaches you can put to use today.

When you have finished reading *Sizzling Sales Ideas*, tell us what you think, or better still, send us some of your sales ideas so that we can share them with other financial advisors. You can drop us a line at *amseka@naifa.org* or call 703-770-8204.

Ayo Mseka
Editor-in-Chief
Advisor Today

FOREWORD

The mathematician Archimedes once said, "Give me a lever long enough and a place to stand, and I can move the world." Most great salespeople understand that concept in a different way. They often say, "Give me one good sales idea, and I can break all records."

The book you hold in your hands has not just one good sales idea, but dozens. And they come not just from one source, but from many—the best in the business. Whether you're looking for a new approach, a new referral technique, what to say to the owner of a small business, how to cross-sell from property and casualty to life insurance, it's all here in this great volume.

These are not gimmicks or tricks. The successful salespeople and industry experts writing in this book are experienced and successful precisely because they do not resort to slick tricks or questionable practices. These are solid ideas that have stood the test of time and client scrutiny. In short, the ideas work because they all reflect an understanding of the psychology of the sale, of the necessity to communicate in words and actions a genuine concern for the prospect.

This book is not designed to be read from front to back. In fact, you may never read all of it. It is designed to help you with an aspect of your career that may be troubling you at the moment. It is also a wonderful road map for growth. You may find yourself reading and rereading particular articles as you gain a deeper understanding of the subtleties of an idea. Or, you may spend time on a particular chapter as you develop your own ideas for entering a new market.

Whatever your needs and goals, *Advisor Today's Sizzling Sales Ideas* is worth its weight in gold. You may not become Archimedes, able to move the world, but with this wonderful little book, you will become a better salesperson who is able to improve his world and that of his clients and prospects.

Happy selling!

David Woods, CLU, ChFC, LUTCF, NAIFA CEO

COMPLIANCE ALERT AND DISCLAIMER

Advisor Today and NAIFA remind readers of *Sizzling Sales Ideas* that it is the reader's responsibility to ensure that the manner in which they solicit and sell insurance and other financial products, and the advertising and sales materials they use, comply with applicable state, federal and NASD/SEC requirements, and the compliance rules of the insurance and other financial services companies they represent.

While *Advisor Today* and NAIFA try to provide accurate information, the accuracy and timeliness of the information in this book is not guaranteed, and the generic nature of this book may conflict with specific, and constantly changing, state and federal regulations and the rules of insurance and other financial services companies. If in doubt about compliance issues, check with your company.

This book does not constitute insurance, financial, investment, tax, legal, accounting or other professional services or advice by *Advisor Today*, NAIFA or the book's contributors. The content of this book represents the views of its respective contributors and does not necessarily reflect the views of *Advisor Today* or NAIFA. *Advisor Today* and NAIFA do not endorse the products or services offered by this book's contributors and disclaim all liability for any claims or damages that may result from the use of this book.

Complying with do not call

As you implement some of the ideas in this book, remember that you must comply with national do-not-call rules. A few reminders:

*If a client or prospect has registered his phone number on the registry, that registration is effective for five years. FCC rules prohibit anyone from making phone solicitations to telephone numbers that are registered in the database, with certain exceptions. These exceptions include tax-exempt nonprofit organizations, political organizations, solicitation calls on behalf of charities and calls to conduct surveys.

*Calls to consumers with whom a business already has an established business relationship are also exempt from the do-not-call rule. An established business relationship exists when the consumer has made a purchase or entered into another transaction with the business within the 18-month period prior to the call or when the consumer has made an inquiry or application to the business within the last three months.

*Each business that makes telephone solicitations must maintain a company-specific, do-not-call list of residential and wireless telephone numbers that includes the telephone number of every person who has asked to be put on the company's do-not-call list. Businesses must process and honor requests to be placed on their do-not-call lists.

*If a telemarketer receives written consent from a consumer including the telephone number that can be called, the telemarketer can make calls to that number, whether or not it is registered on the do-not-call list.

*Calling a residential telephone number with a prerecorded message, blocking caller identification information and making any telemarketing calls between 9 p.m. and 8 a.m. are not allowed.

More information on the national do-not-call registry may be found at *www.fcc.gov/cgb/donotcall.*

PROSPECTING

Let your business prospects see you as a problem solver.

You can accelerate a close if you are perceived as an expert in solving a potential client's problem. Every company, industry or market segment has recurrent and pervasive problems. It is your job to devise a tangible connection between your client's need and your solution, which you personally are able to provide.

Knowing the target market's common issues, you can introduce your solutions just by targeting your questions to industry-specific problems. The expertise you display in solving problems specific to your prospect's industry allows him to see and trust the expertise you have in financial planning. If you are perceived as an expert in solving business problems, you will be perceived as an expert in all the problems your prospect might have—including financial planning.

The best way I have found to penetrate any new or existing market is by clearly defining that market, creating a strategic architecture to capture and maintain that market and becoming an expert in solving the problems in that market. The barriers of resistance and procrastination will melt away once your unspoken credibility is clearly understood. Consider yourself as being "test-driven" without leaving the parking lot.

Dick Zalack is an entrepreneurial strategist who helps sole practitioners or entrepreneurs become better small-business owners, equipping them to take their business to the next level. He can be reached at 330-225-0707 or at www.focusfour. com.

Hold a business-card drawing at an upscale restaurant.

Want a quick and easy way to get a list of the names of businesspeople in your community for the mere cost of one lunch per month? Pick out a fine restaurant that's known for power lunches—where the movers and shakers dine.

Approach the owner and suggest he put a fishbowl in the lobby with a sign directing customers to drop their business cards in for a drawing for a free lunch.

You, of course, will sponsor the lunch. You will also pick up the cards and be glad to provide the restaurant owner with a list of the cards for his own mailing list. This is not a bad group to get in front of, and you can set these up in a number of restaurants around town.

By the way, do not forget about the owners of those restaurants. They need life insurance, too.

Stanley B. Greenfield, RHU, is with Ohio National Life in Jacksonville, Fla. You may reach him at stan@stanleygreenfield.com.

Use attention-grabbing gimmicks.

For all his shyness, insurance sales legend Ben Feldman wasn't above using brash, attention-getting gimmicks. When a prospect repeatedly refused to see him, he would send along five, crisp $100 bills with a note: "I'll trade these for five minutes." Few were able to resist that approach, and no one ever kept the money.

In Feldman's early days, the presentation booklet he took to interviews was a big, leather binder with a real $1,000 bill displayed on the first page. "These come in packages of 100. How many packages do you want?" he would ask.

Thomas John Wolff, CLU, ChFC, served as 1979-1980 president of NALU (NAIFA). A member of MDRT since 1958, he is a recipient of the John Newton Russell Award. He is a member of Hartford AIFA (Conn.). His address is PO Box H, Vernon, CT 06066. You may reach him at 860-875-2591.

Use the following tips to get more prospects.

Insurance agents and financial advisors must continually replenish their sales pipelines. Here are some ideas to help with your prospecting challenges.

1. Expand your relationships. Find out the names of the directors of the companies that you prospect and send each of them free literature or research reports on the products and services you sell. Determine if they are directors of other companies as well. Some may be on several boards. If you can get to one company, you may be able to get to all.

You can obtain this information in several ways. The library has directories of corporate officers and directors. These directories usually cross-reference positions. You can also get information directly from your prospects if they are publicly held corporations.

Action plan: Go the library and locate *America's Families*, the *Directory of Corporate Affiliations*, the *Million Dollar Directory*, and *Owners and Officers of Private Companies*. Also, check the Internet for annual reports.

2. Join Toastmasters. Toastmasters is a terrific organization that has helped many agents and advisors develop poise in front of an audience, and there are local chapters everywhere. In Toastmasters, you will give a series of speeches designed to improve your speaking ability. You will also have the chance to practice speeches and presentations you will give to clients and prospects.

Action plan: Some newspapers have meeting information and you can call 800-993-7732 for the chapter closest to you.

3. Smile. Smile when you call a prospect. It affects your voice through the phone. If you are making a face-to-face sales call, take a minute before you enter the meeting to reaffirm your positive attitude. If you feel good about yourself and your product and expect to make a sale and win a friend, why should you not feel good? Smile and go in.

Maintaining a cheerful attitude is very important. No one wants to deal with a hangdog agent or advisor. You may have just lost a big opportunity but do not let that sour you to the point of losing another. If you think cheerful, you will become cheerful. If you think success, you will find it easier to attain success.

4. Compliment your prospects. Think of ways to compliment prospects about their businesses. This will establish a positive basis for your conversation. It is also a better conversation opener than fishing or baseball because it focuses on business, specifically your prospect's business.

Here are some ideas:

- I was reading your annual report and saw that ...

- I could not help but notice how friendly your employees are. Your company must be great to work for.

- I saw the sign in your lobby that said you have had 432 days without a serious accident. That is pretty impressive.

- I see in the newspaper that you just won a big government contract. Congratulations!

Focus on the prospect and his business, not yours. Never brag about your company's success as a lead-in. If you open with: "Did you see that our profits were up 20 percent last quarter?" how do you think the prospect will react? He will think: "This salesman thinks I'm going to help him get rich. I'll show him."

Action plan: Write down five compliments you can give your clients and prospects.

5. Use a reader-response card. Create your own card, asking questions you want answered. Include this card with everything you mail. Avoid using paper that is heavy enough to cost you additional postage.

A business reply permit costs about $85 per year, and you pay 44 cents plus normal postage for each return piece that is mailed to you. If you anticipate over 500 return pieces per year, the rate structure will be different. Of course, you can let the prospect provide the return postage if you wish, but that will reduce the number of responses you receive.

Consider offering something, such as a research report or a newsletter subscription, to prospects who complete the information you requested.

Action plan: Create your reader-response card.

6. Become a speaker. Offer to speak at a local club such as a Rotary, Lions or Optimist lunch meeting. You can find out when these clubs meet by checking the business pages of the newspaper or calling local restaurants and inquiring what organizations use their meeting rooms. Most civic organizations are generally receptive to outside speakers. These speaking engagements will give you the opportunity to:

- Present yourself in a nonconfrontational manner.

- Deliver a talk that you have prepared well and are entirely at ease in giving.

- Tell them about your service.

Action plan. Look in the business pages of your newspaper for meeting information. Call restaurants and ask if they have a meeting room and who uses it. Ask for contact names and phone numbers and call them.

7. Talk to people you meet in airplanes. Virtually any flight will have you on the plane for an hour or more. That is plenty of time to find out what the passenger next to you and the one on the other side of the aisle do.

If you can, fly first class. My experience is that the first-class cabin is almost always filled with businesspeople using frequent-flyer upgrades. These business executives may include prospects.

Action plan: On your next flight, do not do any paperwork or read a magazine until you have found out what the people next to you and across the aisle do for a living and for whom.

8. Attend networking meetings. Find out where the local chamber of commerce holds a happy hour, breakfast meeting or networking meeting. Attend these meetings and hand out your business card. If your business is with local companies, you will find that these meetings are a valuable source of leads and contacts. Even if the people you meet are not direct prospects, they may know someone who is.

One networking organization that is likely to have a chapter that meets near you is the Leads Club. This national organization has only one purpose—to generate leads for its members. Local clubs are limited to 30 members, none of whom can be from the same industry. Call 800-783-3761 to find the club that is the closest to you.

Also, check the business pages of your local newspaper. You may find other networking meetings, too. These may be privately sponsored. Attending networking meetings will also give you an opportunity to practice your professional social skills. Many of us are comfortable with family and friends but tend to freeze up when we are confronted with new and unfamiliar situations. Here is your chance to overcome that panic.

Action plan: Attend five meetings.

9. Watch other people. When we think about closed and open body language, we typically use hand and arm gestures as examples. Closed gestures are crossed arms or clenched fists. Open gestures are palm-up motions.

Frequently, gestures are displayed in groups. Disinterest may be shown, for example, by a person with crossed arms, crossed legs or rocking back or away from you, with his body turned in a different direction. Matching your visible behavior with that of your prospect may help in establishing rapport. How does the U.S. Army build esprit de corps? By marching in cadence for hours. Watch two friends walking down the street together; unconsciously, they will be walking in step even though one may have longer legs.

In a business interview, if the person you are meeting is laid back while you're intently leaning forward, your behavior may be interpreted as pushy or too intense.

Action plan: Think about how you stand, walk and talk. What do you do with your hands? Is your handshake firm without being overbearing? Do you make good eye contact without being threatening?

Tom Metcalf is a professional speaker and trainer who works with insurance agents and other professionals across the country. His book, Prospecting for Gold, *is published by PSI Research/Oasis Press. Contact him at P.O. Box 670471, Marietta, GA 30066 or* TOMetcalf@aol.com.

Organize your cold-calling process into four steps to boost sales.

Step #1: A wave mailing to targeted prospects

A targeted wave mailing builds recognition, which enables your cold calls to become warmer. After determining that a particular product satisfies a specific need, target your market by purchasing a list of prospects. Stick to a geographic area with one ZIP code. This reduces the cost of bulk mailing and makes your traveling less hectic once you start scheduling appointments. Request that the list be produced on labels and in manuscript form, which should also include phone numbers and addresses. You will want to mail to this list of prospects at least three times using a different mail piece each time.

Reproduce one set of labels for transferring to index cards so that you can write notes on the back of each card whenever you make a contact. These can serve as back-up to entries made in your computerized contact management software program.

Step #2: Cold calling

Once the mailing campaign has gone through at least three separate cycles, phone call follow-up should begin. Over the years, we have collected a number of phone scripts that follow this outline:

1. Salutation

2. Who we are and where we are from

3. Request to speak to a specific person

4. Reason for the call

5. Asking for an appointment

6. Handling objections

7. Restatement of appointment date and time

8. Thank you and close

Step #3: Handling objections

We have a collection of objections and replies. Whenever we hear a new objection, we add it to our collection, along with a reply that addresses the objection.

Because of compliance issues, we maintain a do-not-call list, which we keep updated.

Step #4: Keeping records

A telephone activity results form is used each day to track success by comparing the number of calls dialed to the number of results. Our incentive comes from the realization that each time a number is dialed, it is worth a certain amount of commission, regardless of whether it results in an appointment.

Once we schedule an appointment, we update the index card, along with entries in our contact management software program. Because our office computers are networked, everyone in the office views the appointment schedule.

Although cold calling is an art, it can also be a science if you set up systems in your office to help organize the entire process. By making the process mechanical and repetitious, you reduce the solicitor's fear of picking up the phone.

Jeffrey T. Wilkie, LUTCF, of New Rochelle, N.Y., has been an agent and registered representative in the insurance and investment-planning arena for the past 15 years. He can be reached at 888-616-5656.

Complete a project 30 at the beginning of each month.

Most life insurance producers had to complete a project 100 prior to starting in life insurance sales. Over the years, I have found it motivating and rewarding to do a project 30 at the beginning of each month. These 30 names are the names of potential people who could be sold something in a coming month. The project can include all opened cases, pending closing cases, term conversions, age changes, put-offs to a later date, annual policy reviews and hot prospects.

List the name, phone number, type of sale, potential premium and potential commission. I find that usually one-third of the cases listed will be sold during the month, and one-sixth of the premiums projected are closed. Having the anticipated sales and projected results in front of you will help focus your attitude.

Bill Martin of Mutual Service Corp. in Tampa, Fla., can be reached at 813-287-2148.

Include your product and service information in the Welcome Wagon.

I signed a contract with the Welcome Wagon to be included in the basket of material that goes to each new arrival in the neighborhood. It costs me $2 every time they deliver a basket. For a new homeowner, I provide a welcome letter and a pencil that has my name and address on it. For new parents, I provide a congratulatory letter and a baby spoon, also with my name and address.

At the end of each month, the local Welcome Wagon representative sends me the names and phone numbers of everyone she has contacted so that I can follow up. I get to see a good number of people from this, many of whom I sell products and services.

*John A. Hamilton, CLU, of Hamilton Financial Services
in Duxbury, Mass., can be reached at 781-934-6115 or*
hamins@idt.net.

Learn how to let your mailer work as hard as you do.

If you want people to buy more, they need to know what you offer. But if you've mailed clients and prospects information on what you do and the services you provide, don't make the mistake of assuming they now understand you. The flaw with this is that most direct mail is never even opened, let alone read.

If you want to increase sales, you need to make your mailer interesting so it will get read. Here are a couple of ways to cut through the clutter of everyone else's marketing messages and get noticed.

- Remember that size does matter. As a matter of fact, the size of your mailer can have a huge impact on whether your target market reads your message. Invitation-size envelopes and large 9x12-inch envelopes generate the highest reader-ship because they stand out and get opened.

- Involve the reader. One way to involve the reader is to ask questions in the mailer. This will lead to more sales.

Remember that if you want to increase your sales, your mailer must work as hard as you do.

Martin R. Baird is president of Advisor Marketing, an Annapolis, Md.-based consulting firm, and author of The 7 Deadly Sins of Advisor Marketing. *You may reach him at* mbaird@advisormarketing.com *or 480-991-6420.*

Increase sales by increasing exposure.

The old adage that sales is a numbers game is true in many ways. To increase sales, more people need to know what you do and how you can help them. Getting your message out to the news media can have a huge impact on your sales success.

To get media attention, review your strong marketing message and present it to reporters, editors and producers in a newsworthy way.

When I say a strong message, I mean that it needs to be about solu-tions that the readers or viewers are looking for. The more news-worthy it is, the more willing the media will be to share it with their audience. Here's a secret that's good to know—including a photo-graph can increase the likelihood your information will get published or aired. Sending out one simple press release that's published in the right place for your target market could create the sales boost that you are looking for.

Martin R. Baird is president of Advisor Marketing, an Annapolis, Md.-based consulting firm, and author of The 7 Deadly Sins of Advisor Marketing. *You may reach him at* mbaird@advisormarketing.com *or 480-991-6420.*

Use your current centers of influence to help cross over into a new market.

In the mid-1980s, a resourceful television hero named MacGyver emerged. Week to week he would turn weed killer into a bomb, hot-wire a car with a paper clip and power a transistor radio with the electrolytes from cactus juice. He was the poor man's James Bond, using the limited resources he had, but achieving Bond-like results.

Often, our limited resources are enough to allow us to reach our goals if we use them in a slightly different way. Take the problem of advisors who want to upgrade their markets but do not have access to prospects in those markets. How can they gain access? The answer may very well lie within their relationships in their current natural markets. They simply need a strategy.

You usually use centers of influence to identify prospects in a market. You can, however, use your current COIs to identify COIs in a new target market.

According to one life insurance company's district sales manager who uses this technique successfully, when you begin prospecting in a new market, generating prospects is more important than making immediate sales. Trying to make a sale immediately may jeopardize the relationship and cut you off from what you really need—more prospects. Let's look at one way to use your current COIs to break into new markets.

First, define the new target market clearly. You should identify the common characteristics of the new market. These include the prospects' ages, incomes, marital status, assets and occupations. Take the time to write these items down in a profile that you can clearly communicate to the COI. The more specific you are, the easier it will be for your COI to help you. For example, "people earning $50,000 to $75,000 annually" may not be as easy to identify as "people who work as civil engineers, electrical engineers, computer programmers and so forth."

Second, make a list of people (and their phone numbers) in your natural market that you think can help you as a COI. They need to meet four criteria:

- They know you.

- They like you.

- They trust you.

- They are willing to help you.

Third, call each COI on your list. Tell him: "I need your help." When we hear the word help, something inside us causes us to want to help if we can. Tell the COI what you want. For example, you can say: "I would like to meet with you for 15 to 20 minutes to see if you might be able to help me expand my market." If he is busy, offer to buy breakfast or lunch.

Fourth, when you meet with him, present the list of your new target market's common characteristics.

Fifth, once your COI gives you the names of the people in your target market, ask him for information about each person. Where does he

live? What organizations does he belong to? How old are his children? Ask for any information you need.

Sixth, ask your COI to tell the people he recommends that you will be contacting them. This could be in the form of a phone call, a letter or an email. Have examples of what to say in case you are asked. If your COI cannot commit to this, ask to use his name when you contact the prospect. Without this, you do not have a warm lead; you have a cold call.

Finally, contact the person your COI has recommended. Here is the twist: You are not going to approach the person as a prospect but as a COI. Your approach may sound like this: "Hello, John, this is Joe Smith from XYZ Insurance. Mary Jones recommended that I talk to you. I need your help. I would like to get together to show you the type of work that I can do for people who are in your situation. My intention is not to sell you anything; instead, I would like to introduce myself and see if you might know of people who might benefit from the work that I do."

When you meet with each person, explain what you do and demonstrate the value you create for people like him. Then ask him for referrals, using the same common characteristics you used with your original COI. Again, obtain as much information as you can about each referred lead.

This method of prospecting is simple. Sometimes the easiest twist of a tried-and-true prospecting concept can open the path to an otherwise closed market. As the old saying goes, when you cannot find a door, look for a window. All you need is a way in.

Kirk Okumura is an LUTC author and editor with The American College. You can reach him at kirko@amercoll. edu.

When holding seminars for worksite marketing, focus on education, not on products.

When holding a seminar for worksite marketing, try to begin the conversation by explaining how financial education can benefit a small-business owner and his firm. Get the owner to see your service as a value-added benefit. If you position yourself as someone who specializes in financial education, you are more likely to capture the owner's attention. Employers and employees are interested in education, not products.

Although it's important to provide full disclosure regarding your financial practice, the language you use is just as critical. Present yourself as someone who provides financial education as the focus of your practice.

While education is important, owners want to know that you can alleviate their fears about employee seminars. At the top of the list is the concern that you will pressure employees to do business with you.

One way to overcome this perception is not to take an aggressive approach. Assure the employer that you will only contact an employee after the seminar if that employee requests you do so. Explain how the employee should make this request, usually by completing an evaluation form or a factfinder. To reassure the employer, offer to put this promise in writing. This will make him feel more comfortable with the idea of your conducting a seminar.

What types of businesses should you solicit? I recommend approaching small to medium-sized organizations, with a minimum of 100 employees. This ensures you get a reasonable audience for your initial presentation, which is crucial if you are to continue your relationship with the employer.

You may feel like going after large companies, but the General Electrics and General Motors of the world are inundated with pitches by financial advisors. The chance of getting in the door of a large employer is small. And even if you are lucky enough to succeed, it usually takes more than a year for you to get approved as a vendor.

Also, try prospecting beyond the private sector. Approach public-sector employers and professional associations. These groups are often underserved by financial advisors, especially in the area of financial education.

Not everyone on the company's payroll will fit your client profile. Although it is not possible to screen attendees, there are ways to attract the types of people you are interested in. Start by approaching firms that hire the type of client you prefer. Professional associations are a good source. Infiltrating a medical association, for example, may result in your getting the type of client you want.

You can also segment the employee population within one company. For example, conduct a presentation for the rank-and-file employees and a separate, higher-level presentation for management. This will help you provide added value to the people you want as clients.

Jeff Franz is president of FMT Solutions, a coaching service in Tucson, Ariz. Contact him at jeff@fmtsolutions.com. *(*www.fmtsolutions.com*)*

Use other people's eyes and ears to get new prospects.

If you are visiting or having an interview in an office building, stop for a few minutes and note the name of the businesses near your client or prospect.

During the conversation with your client, just ask him in passing if he knows any of his office neighbors. If he says yes, ask him: "What can you tell me about him?" Another approach might be: "I notice that John Prospect works in this building. Have you met him?"

As your client talks, take the information down and ask about another. The number of people you can ask about will depend on how good a memory you have for names and numbers.

Office-directory prospecting is one of the easiest ways I know to meet new people who can use our services. It is a case of using other people's eyes and ears.

William David Barnes of Barnes and Co. Inc., in Tampa, Fla., can be reached at 813-968-6181 or at barnesandco@aol.com.

When meeting with your client, ask how you can help him.

One of the best ways I have found to create a relationship and maintain it is by leading (or following up) with a service approach. Early in discussions with my prospects, I ask them the following questions:

1. What are your current plans, and are your beneficiary designations current?

2. Do you have an older universal life policy ready to implode because it was set up on higher interest earnings that have not prevailed?

3. Is the ownership of the policy still correct?

4. Are dividend options suitable to your situation?

This approach not only begins a dialogue with the prospect; it also shows I have an interest in looking beyond an immediate sale. I am creating a mood that suggests to him that he needs me.

In an effort to follow through with my clients, I meet with them annually to see what has changed since we last met. When a trust level is already established, possibilities will develop.

It is important to ask your clients and prospects this question: "How can I help you today?" This will give them an opportunity to discuss whatever financial concerns or interests they might have.

James R. Fenner, LUTCF, of Fenner Financial Advisors, can be reached at 970-223-4323.

Look to yourself first.

The best sales starter I can recommend is to look at your own program. Is it adequate? Have you considered all the contingencies? Have you looked at all your possible needs?

Depending on your age and financial situation, this could be life insurance for protection or estate liquidity. It could mean disability income or long-term care insurance. It could be Medicare supplement, a cancer policy, hospital indemnity or other medical care supplement coverage.

If your coverage is adequate, you know the questions your prospect needs to answer to know if his coverage is adequate. If it is not and you choose not to do anything about it, you will know the objections you have to overcome (although my guess is that if you cannot overcome them for yourself, you will not be able to overcome those from your prospect).

But if you recognize your shortfall and correct it, you will have a powerful story to share with your prospect. Prospects want to be thoughtful and make the right decision. If you show them how you concluded you had a shortfall and solved it, often, they will do the same thing. We lead best by example. It is also easier for prospects to follow us, knowing that this is the road we, as knowledgeable travelers, took. Take the high road and insure yourself.

Howard M. Rosenblatt, J.D., CLU, of Mutual of New York in Gainesville, Fla., can be reached at 352-373-7100 or howard_rosenblatt@mony.com.

Let your clients help you find prospects.

This is one of those sales ideas that once you try it, it works so well that you might stop doing it. That would be a shame because this is a technique that could, if consistently used, take your career to another level and end your prospecting woes forever.

As you know, the annual review is a great way to "show and tell" your clients how their programs are doing at solving the problems you pointed out previously. At the annual review, you are truly doing your clients a service, following through on what you promised. They are likely to be happy that you have kept your promise to be of service. You would think that this would be the most likely time to obtain referrals to those people about whom your client is most concerned or respects the most.

Typically, somewhere near the end of your annual review meeting, you would ask your client: "Do you know someone in a similar situation that I should call on to explain what I do?" (You could insert your own referral-question language here.) The bottom line is that you ask for referrals in a way that is comfortable for you and that you think will elicit a positive response from your client. Typically, your client's answer would be some variation of this: "I cannot think of anyone right off the top of my head, but if I do, I will be sure to give you a call."

This is not the response you want. Next time, try something a little more imaginative. Before your annual review meeting, prepare a prompting list of people in the same social circle, country club, avocation, occupation, related business, neighborhood, alumni group or whatever. The list should have at least 25 names on it. It would be pretty cool if you had the people's addresses and telephone numbers, too.

When the natural time comes for you to ask for referrals, show your client the list of the names of people you want to call on and ask for his help in steering you to them. This exercise will be much less stressful for your client, and you will have a ready-made reason to ask him about the people on the list. You will not believe the difference.

Side benefit: With more referred leads come more sales, better persistency, higher first-year commissions and larger persistency bonuses. These are good things.

Charles W. Potts, CLU, RHU, is with MassMutual Financial Group in Oklahoma City, Okla. He can be reached at 405-270-8000 or charlie@charliepotts.com.

Do an insurance audit for your clients.

You have to be a good educator to be a good salesman. One of the best ways to educate your clients is by using analogy. Here is one for breaking down sales resistance in the business market.

"I know you are sincere when you say you have done some planning, Mr. Businessman. I assume you have a company treasurer or comptroller. Am I right? And am I right in also assuming that you have an outside firm of independent CPAs who periodically audit your books?

This is done not to check up on your own people but simply to determine whether some of your procedures might be improved. Perhaps your depreciation schedule might be modified or your billing methods changed. And this periodic audit of your books makes good business sense, doesn't it?

"This same approach can be helpful in your business insurance planning. We would like to come in as an outside firm of independent auditors and simply audit your business' insurance portfolio. We may be able to come up with some practical suggestions that will save you money. And if we do have some ideas that prove helpful, we would hope to be given credit for those ideas and permitted to represent your interests in implementing them. Do you see how any of this could hurt you?"

Curt B. Ford, J.D., ChFC, of Northwestern Mutual of Mill Valley, Calif., can be reached at 415-383-5277.

When you are new in town, use the loss-leader approach.

As a new agency in our city, we struggled to compete against the already established agencies and agents in the area. By using a loss-leader approach widely used in the retail industry, we have been able to establish exceptional results in the business market as well as the personal market. This approach stems from providing unique products that your competition is not willing to offer generally because the commissions are very low.

We began with a dental plan that we offered for $23.45 per month for an individual, or $60 per month for a family. We advertised this service in a thrifty nickel column in those weekly papers you find at the supermarket. We ran this ad in each of those papers in Idaho for three months at a cost of about $100 per month. The result was an average of six calls a day. Mondays were the best, with a record of 14 calls.

When people responded, we explained the dental plan and offered to either mail them literature or meet with them. During the conversation, we began to gather information about the prospect. This was information we would use later to accomplish the one thing many agents either forget or neglect to do: cross-sell. With this information, we asked if they would like to know more about our products, such as health and life insurance. The most impressive sale we made from this three-month run was to a person who came to the office and not only purchased my $23.45 per month dental plan, but also a $100,000 annuity a week later.

In the business market, we use a group dental plan that can offer orthodontic coverage for groups of two or more people. The rates are more competitive than the rates of any of the carriers we have run up against. The company also offers a voluntary dental plan for groups of three people or more, and it is able to attach a vision plan with the dental through an agreement with the company.

Because the product is unique, we receive many inquiries and have been able to establish many group life, health and short- and long-term disability plans. Traditionally, most dental carriers require a minimum of 25 employees to offer orthodontia.

I can't say enough about cross-selling. How much money do agents leave behind on the table every week? I would not even want to know.

Lance B. Kolbet is with University Financial Group
in Pucatello, Idaho. Contact him at 208-234-1800.

Make those telephone calls.

My best all-purpose sales idea is telephone activity.

Challenge yourself to make a specific number of phone calls each week to prospects. And make those calls regardless of any and all circumstances. If you run out of good prospects, call the not-so-good ones. This activity will force you to improve the process of getting good ones.

This idea will work only if the number of calls you need to make exceeds the number of calls you were making before you realized you needed a new sizzling sales idea.

> *John A. Styer, CLU, ChFC, LUTCF, of New York Life in North East, Md., can be reached at 410-287-8844 or* jstyer@ft.newyorklife.com.

With a little planning, better cold-calling results could be a ring away.

When calling prospects, are you reading a script? Surfing the Internet? Talking between sips of coffee? For most brokers, cold calling means simply picking up the phone and dialing the next name on a list. But you wouldn't meet a prospect in person without preparing, so why treat phone calls as any less important? Fortunately, a few minutes of forethought and planning can go a long way toward improving your success in this area.

Prepare

As with other aspects of the business, there's a skill set to using the telephone more effectively. Before you ever pick up the phone, here are some things you should always do to prepare:

- Do a "check-in" with yourself. Determine how you're feeling both physically and mentally. What is your physical state? Most importantly, assess your energy level. It's essential that you come to the phone with plenty of energy because it will carry over into your conversations.

- Have a clear reason for contacting these people. What is the goal of your call? Are you trying to get appointments or seeking decisions on a particular product? Many brokers make the crucial mistake of calling simply to send out information to the prospect. Investors pick up on this, and half the time people will request your information just to get off the phone. When this happens, you'll mistakenly think you're better off than you are in terms of interested prospects. What is more important, you waste valuable time. Rather than working to get qualified investors, you'll spend hours following up on prospects—many of whom won't be interested.

- Make your primary goal setting up a meeting. It's OK to send information to prospects who are genuinely interested, but don't let that be your dominant goal.

- Finally, it's essential to communicate as if this person were sitting in front of you. Your physiology, or body language, has to be excellent, since that will come through just as your energy does. To better do this, I offer two recommendations: First, if you're not using a headset, you're losing money. Try it and you'll see what I mean. Second, do prospecting calls standing up. By using your body, you'll sound better and have better rapport with the person on the other end.

Communicate

Another important aspect to improving your cold calling is to recognize the three modes of communication and understand how they rank in importance.

- Words (What are you going to say? What are you going to ask?)

- Voice quality and inflection (talking softly, speaking quickly)

- Physiology (body language)

In order of importance, your physiology is the top method of communication. Voice quality comes in second, while the actual words you use are the least important. This may sound surprising, but if you're following a script and not getting results, then you have the order backwards.

Prospect

Once you have the individual on the phone, here are some steps that will improve your chances.

- Introduce yourself in the first five to 10 seconds and ask a question that requires more than a one-word answer. "Do you have a moment to speak with me?" usually works. Listen to the person's voice and match it. Pay attention to his pace, rhythm and volume. People often respond favorably to someone who is like them and matching their voice builds rapport. Avoid launching into a speech, since it almost never works.

- Many people ask: "What's in it for me?" When that happens, say something different: "Have you had your financial plan updated in the last six months?" "Have you sat down with your advisor in the last 90 days?" Ask something that brings a question to their mind. When they respond, be curious. "Did they make any new recommendations?" "What kind of investor are you?" Deal with objections by asking a question.

- Within the first minute, create a compelling reason for this person to continue talking to you. Remember, people are motivated by their needs—not yours. Almost every investor needs a portfolio review, risk-tolerance analysis or asset-allocation model, and 90 percent of investors haven't had that done. Or ask about their relationship with their broker.

- Take the pressure off by being up-front. For example, you can say: "I'm not calling to sell you anything. I just would like to find out if there is a way I can help you." This is essential because the person at the other end is in a defensive mode.

- To qualify yourself without being intrusive, say: "I tend to work with people that have at least $100,000 to $150,000 minimum in investment. I understand that describes your situation." Follow up with: "I'd like to find a time we can get together and go over your situation. What's the best day for you next week?"

- Never use the word appointment. The word usually creates a negative connotation. (When was the last time you looked forward to a doctor's appointment?) Instead, ask: "Why don't we pick out a time to look over your situation?"

- Be prepared to counter if the prospect wavers. Remain relaxed. "Wouldn't it be worth 30 minutes to 45 minutes of your time to find out what your asset allocation should be?" Expect objections. Ask, "Wouldn't it be worth X or Y to get together?"

- Don't use the word "but." Doing so breaks rapport and creates confrontation. The word often signifies disagreement with what the other person has said, so use the words: "And didn't you say ..." or, "And wouldn't it be worth ..."

- Use the word "because." When you ask a prospect for something, the first thing he does is to ask himself: "Why do I want to do this?" By using the word "because" with a list of compelling reasons, you help prospects answer the questions they are already asking themselves.

While no two prospects are alike, you can take advantage of these tips and suggestions to improve your success when cold calling. Soon they'll be a regular part of your routine.

Joseph J. Lukacs, practice strategist and coach, is the founder of International Performance Group LLC. Since 1993, Lukacs has been delivering customized individual coaching by telephone to financial and insurance professionals. He is also available for speaking engagements on a limited basis. International Performance Group LLC is based in Melbourne, Fla. He can be reached at 321-255-2889 or jjl@ipgllc.com, or by visiting his website, www.ipgllc.com.

Put yourself in your prospect's shoes.

If you want to effectively sell your professional services, begin by psychologically projecting yourself into the shoes of your prospective client.

Here is the problem you face from the consumer's point of view. Let us say I am the consumer. Now, if I want to buy a product, I have a number of ways to evaluate the product. I can touch it, taste it, take it for a test drive and if I do not like it, return it and get my money back. Moreover, when I buy the product, I take control of it.

On the other hand, when I buy a professional service, I face a number of fear-inducing problems. First, I am buying something invisible and intangible. Second, the only way I can properly evaluate the service is after it has been performed. Third, I am buying the service from someone I do not know. Fourth, I am paying a significant fee or some part of it, in advance. Fifth, I am buying in a field in which I have no knowledge or expertise. Sixth, instead of taking control, I am handing over control—and in an area of vital importance in my life, perhaps second only to my health.

So, Mr. Advisor, I am sitting across the desk from you, scared out of my mind and feeling a large gap in comfort, trust and confidence.

Addressing that gap is the key step in your sales effort. Without addressing this issue, every sale will be a struggle. Worse, it will be a struggle that you will have to repeat with each client.

The typical professional seeks to address this gap with education. The strategy is to say these words to himself: "I have this great process, product or experience … the potential client will rationally evaluate all of this and choose me."

The problem is that this strategy is based on a false premise that the buying decision is a rational decision. It is not.

For one thing, the potential client has no rational basis on which to base his decision. He does not have any expertise in financial matters. You sound very convincing, but so do all of the other advisors.

So here is the truth that you will ignore at your peril. The buying decision is not a rational decision; it is an emotional process. For most of my clients, the preferred method of gaining clients is through refer-

P R O S P E C T I N G

rals. That is because business that is referred to them comes, in effect, presold. That key question—of trust, comfort, liking—is more than halfway answered. They have third-party credibility. In the same way, marketing can make the sales process easier. The prospect has already heard of you, has read your article, been to your seminar, seen your ad and visited your website. Act as if your prospect is already your client.

But we will assume that the prospect is in your office, regardless of how he got there. How do your sell him? How do you "close" him?

Keeping in mind our admonition that the purchase will be an emotional one and that you are in a relationship business, I advocate the following: Proceed as if each prospect is already your client.

I advise my clients that the goal of a consultation is not to come away with a contract, a retainer or a check. The goal is to bond emotionally with the potential client. The goal is to form a relationship.

If your potential client comes out of that meeting and says: "Wow, that John Jones is the nicest guy I ever met," I promise you, Mr. Jones, that you will have more sales than you can handle. One of the aspects of your attitude that will strongly communicate itself is how you feel about the meeting and how you are going to behave if the prospect leaves your office without committing—or even turns you down flat.

When I was about 12 years old, I sent in a response card that provoked a visit from a salesman for *Encyclopedia Britannica*. The man met with my bemused parents and me, and made a wonderful presentation. But my parents were not ready to shell out several hundred dollars for something that was accessible free of charge in the public library.

"I am sorry for wasting your time," I said to the man. He smiled. "I am never wasting my time when I am talking about *Encyclopedia Britannica*," he said.

I was enormously impressed—even at age 12—and about a year later, we wound up buying the full set of encyclopedias from the salesman. Some 49 years later, my sister still has them.

There is a bit of Zen in this approach: Try not to be too "outcome oriented." I am a fairly passionate golfer and not a bad one. But like many golfers—especially as they get older—the part of the game that gave me the most trouble was putting. I tried mallet putters and blade putters and belly putters. Nothing worked.

And then one day I read a bit of advice that made all the difference. The writer said I should not worry so much about the outcome and should devote myself to the process. This means that if I did all the things I was supposed to do—such as lining up correctly, holding my head still and putting a good stroke on the ball—that was a good putt. Some would go in the hole and some would miss, but that was not my worry. My job was to hit a good putt and let the putts fall as they may.

Immediately, every putt became a positive experience for me. I enjoyed trying to put my best stroke on it, and I was not traumatized when the putt did not go in. If I hit a good putt, then I considered myself successful, regardless of whether or not it dropped in the hole.

Of course, as soon as I adopted this attitude, my muscles were relaxed, my breathing was calm, my mind was focused—and many more of my putts started dropping.

Likewise, I would advise you to be process-oriented in your sales presentations. If you have presented your services well and have bonded emotionally, you have "made a good putt." You have been successful. Some will become your clients and some will not, but all can be your friends and advocates.

*Mark Merenda is president of Smart Marketing in Naples,
Fla. Contact him at 239-403-7755.*

31

APPROACH

Present yourself as a radio broadcaster.

One way to make more sales is to present yourself, your message and your personality as if you are a radio broadcaster. The first thing you learn in radio is how to attract an audience. Warmth, presence, personality, music, talk and information are the elements that make listeners tune into one radio show instead of the other, and this goes for financial advisors, too.

Learn the art of the 60-second commercial. Today, most people get their consumer and financial information over the radio and via the television in 10-, 15-, 30- or 60-second bites. For this reason, you have one minute to tell your story.

You need to shrink your message and your approach into a short, emotionally rich message to get people's attention, keep their interest and lead them to buy your product.

Try this: When you call a prospect and get voice mail, you're usually prompted to leave a message. When that happens, consider yourself on the air. It's time for the One-Minute Show starring you. If you're boffo, the prospect will call back. There is power in knowing that you can honestly say to a prospect, "My presentation will take one minute."

Stan Hustad heads the PTM Group, a Minneapolis-based firm that helps financial professionals effectively market themselves. Contact him at 612-729-0420 or ptmark@aol.com, or through the PTM Group website, www.ptmgroup.com.

Make it personal.

For 15 years, Van Mueller, a registered representative with New England Financial, hated what he did for a living—selling insurance. His career had hit rock bottom, and then a transitional moment took place. He got fired. But some people in the industry thought he was worth saving and said, "Try it this way. Find a way to take care of your customers, and whether you make a sale or not, you'll be a success."

That was the first year he made the Million Dollar Round Table. He now approaches his work with a joyous, almost missionary, zeal. He says that he has information that can change a prospect's life, and that has changed his life. "I never had trouble getting in front of people, but when I got there, I'd get blown away a lot. Now I sit in front of them and talk about what matters," he explains.

He has reached this level in his career through several steps:

- **Practice and listen:** Despite a constant stream of referrals, he practices cold calling to "keep sharp." He also constantly rehearses his sales presentation, which leads to confidence in front of a prospect. Because advisors are too busy thinking of what to say next, most miss when a prospect says something important. "Go make 150 presentations to friends and then ask if they would buy from you. Agents tell me they've improved their careers immediately by doing this because they could spend more time listening," he says.

- **Use emotion:** Get prospects emotionally involved and they'll beg you to buy, Mueller stresses. He does this by warning prospects about what he dubs the three paradigm shifts: People are living longer; the government is not able to take care of the elderly; and the job market is changing due to the transition from an industrial to an information age. "The goal is to get them to understand they won't be able to depend on anyone else," he says. "I use this presentation to get people to tell others about me, so I don't have to ask for referrals, and I use it to close the sale."

- **Create a relationship:** By the end of the presentation, often after an hour or two in a prospect's home, a counselor/friend relationship has developed. "They no longer care about the products; they care about the relationship. Eventually they give me control of their financial lives," he says.

(Reported by Lynn Vincent, contributor to Advisor Today*)*

Tell your story.

Telling stories is one of my favorite sales techniques. They run from saving goose eggs (for selling insurance) to baking cakes (explaining the benefits of long-term investing). These stories make clients laugh, but they also simplify the complexities of personal finance.

For the reluctant prospect, I use my "money dump" close. I lay thousands of dollars on a high-net-worth prospect's desk, and sweep piles onto the floor, representing what would be lost to taxes if she died without proper estate-planning products. I've never had a person buy the day I did that, but I've sold everybody within a year. I think they get nightmares, waking up and seeing that pile of money dropping to the floor.

E. Dennis Zahrbock, CFP, ChFC, CLU, is in business, estate and retirement planning with Business & Estate Advisers, Inc., in Wayzata, Minn. You may reach him at 952-475-0440.

Ask prospects for their agenda early on in a meeting.

When I start an interview, I always have an agenda. But I have found that if I stop at a point early in the interview and say to the prospect: "Look, I have an agenda, but I thought it might be more productive before we get started if you would give me your agenda for this meeting. What do you hope to get from this meeting?"

The prospect then begins talking. He becomes relaxed and opens up. Before you know it, he has laid out the interview for you, telling you exactly what he wants to be sold. This is a sure shortcut to the close.

Richard Brunsman, CLU, ChFC, is with Union Central Life in Cincinnati. Contact him at 513-621-7907 or richard@one.net.

FACTFINDING

Shrink think.

Financial consultant Susan G. Zimmerman says producers can be more successful if they understand consumers' internal conflicts regarding life insurance—and insurance advisors. First, life insurance forces people to think about and plan for their own deaths. Second, life insurance products are many, varied and sometimes seem to conflict with each other. Finally, advisors can create conflict when they sell and advise by pigeonholing—narrowing clients' focus on products the advisors favor and criticizing those they don't.

She suggests that producers practice what she calls "shrink think"—thinking like a therapist. "Point out these conflicts to clients before a solution is ever presented. Ask to what extent they want to look at life insurance, what they have heard about different types of insurance, and whether they believe they've been 'burned' by one type or another." Then, Zimmerman says, listen carefully to a client's priorities, biases and historical preferences. Help him understand his conflicts so he can make informed choices, and be prepared with firm reasoning when another advisor comes in to try to change his mind.

(Reported by Lynn Vincent, contributor to Advisor Today*)*

Prompt your prospects to think.

Here are five simple questions that will prompt your prospects to think about their situations, share their stories and identify their concerns. These questions will get you beyond the facts to the stories that lead to productive presentations.

1. What would happen to you if you were in the hospital for three days?

Here, you help your prospects think about the risks of life and the potential costs. You will learn that most have life insurance already; you can congratulate them on that. You may also discover with whom they are insured, their coverage and whether it is a workplace benefit. You might ask them what their experience has been with health-care issues, coverage and service. Listen for the stories.

2. What would happen to you if you were without a salary or paycheck for three months?

Most people think wheelchairs when they hear the word "disability." They don't see that happening to them. The term "income protection" is better but has little emotional connection. Yet, when people have to think about no pay for three months, they often tell some stories to you and to themselves about their situations and apprehensions. Listen for their fears.

3. What would happen to your family and your business if you were dead for three years?

This question is a chance for some humor and serious conversation at the same time. Ask it with a straight face and a touch of a smile. It may produce a chuckle, a quizzical look or the question, "What do you mean, dead for three years? You're dead forever."

Here you lighten it up and say: "Well, I like to stick with the number three, so let's just say you only have to be dead for three years. Would you have the resources and the means for your family and your business to get through that time until you come back?"

The creative advisor can ask lots of follow-up discovery questions. We discover that most people don't have the resources to get through three years. Listen for the stories, the plans, the apprehensions and the confusion.

4. When do you think you will die?

This question has to be asked with grace, concern and intense listening. This is vital because people, in general, expect to live a long life. The speculations, the concerns, the health issues and the family histories can come pouring out. It is possible that the conversation will cross over to investment hopes from insurance issues. Listen—for their thoughts, their family histories, their expectations and their deep concerns.

5. What do you hope to accomplish before you die?

This final question moves people from fears into hopes, dreams and aspirations. You hear about children's education, retirement plans, starting a business, buying a new home, a summer lake home, a vacation. Prospects tell you what is really important to them—sometimes without realizing it. People do not have strong financial goals; they have personal, emotional goals, and money is just a way to help them achieve them.

When you get only the money facts, you simply have fears without vision. This leaves the door open for you. For example, a 35-year-old expects to live to 85 and retire at 55. The question then is: "How do you plan to do that?" With good prompting, you discover the causes and charities he values. You discover the levels of generosity in his life. You discover what he hopes to do with his business. Without even directly asking him what he values, you help him discover what is truly important to him.

You are now in a position to make statements based on their stories.

"It seems to me that you are very concerned about your children's education. Should we take care of that issue right now?"

"You really want to give a good deal of money to your place of worship. Would you like to make sure that we take care of that now at half the cost and save money on taxes, too?"

"You seem to be concerned about missing a paycheck due to a loss of income or your ability to work. Should we take care of that right now?"

"You want to make sure that your spouse does not have to work or lower her standard of living for at least 10 years should you die unexpectedly. There is a way we can take care of that right now."

Learn to tell your story in one minute, and then ask the questions that allow your prospects to tell their stories. You will get the stories behind the facts—the stories that lead people to make their choices for improving their lives and insuring their futures.

> *Stan Hustad is the leader of the PTM Group. He can be reached at 612-729-0420, ptmark@aol.com or through his website at www.ptmgroup.com.*

Ask your prospects the following questions.

J.A. Abels, an independent broker-dealer in Omaha, Neb., has developed a seven-question, needs-analysis technique designed to determine what prospects want to do about funeral expenses, liquidity, paying off debts (including the mortgage), college education and survivor income. He doesn't ask these seven questions once, however, but several times. This requires the prospects to analyze what their situation would be at various life stages.

"I ask them to look at their needs right now; then I ask them to project to the time when their youngest child would be 16 years old, because that's when a Social Security payment would stop for the surviving spouse, as well as the individual," Abels explains. "Finally, I ask them to pretend they're 65 today, the kids are educated and the house is paid for. Posing the same questions, I help them calculate the amount of money they would need at that time. That gives me a three-plot profile over their lifetime for their assumed need for life insurance. In turn, that helps me determine what combinations of policies and the amounts they need to have in place now and in the future. This kind of analysis also provides an occasion to recommend disability income insurance and long-term care coverage."

(Reported by George A. Norris, former senior editor of Advisor Today)

Try the scratch pad approach.

Bill Hall is an agent with New York Life in Towson, Md., who primarily works the family market, writing between 120 and 150 whole life applications per year. He completes most of his sales within one or two interviews. His is essentially a human life value method, using the sales techniques espoused by New York Life's legendary Ben Feldman.

"I just use a scratch pad, writing down the figures as I try to find out where the prospects are coming from, their incomes and what they feel their needs are, without my telling them how much insurance they ought to have," he says. "It really works very well."

Hall says that a detailed, capital-needs approach isn't necessary in his market, where "these sales are basically common sense, dealing with their current situation and their goals for the future. If you're talking about $100 or less a month in premium, it's not even a two-interview sale, and it doesn't require a complex analysis. In these sales, you want to keep it as simple as possible. Breadwinner prospects simply want you to show them a way to protect their families and save a little money for themselves. Remember, it's what they want, not what you want."

(Reported by George A. Norris, former senior editor of Advisor Today)

Find a need.

While it is important to use the factfinding period to establish a more personal relationship with a prospect—it's vital for earning and retaining a prospect's business—many advisors overlook the basic objective of a factfinder: to lead you to a sale. That doesn't mean creating a need where there isn't one; it means uncovering problems that may not be readily apparent to the client, but need to be resolved eventually. For instance, determining beneficiaries on a life policy for a senior couple with five kids is easy until you find out that two of the kids are remarried with kids from previous marriages. One runs the family business and the other has a substance abuse problem. The couple obviously wants to include each of their kids, but at what cost to their legacy? I can help the couple avoid potentially huge problems such as disinheriting grandchildren and/or leaving undesirable spouses of their own children in the will. The key to discovering these needs is to allow the prospect to discuss his life situation in a nonthreatening environment. Chances are, the prospect doesn't even know he is revealing issues that can affect his estate planning.

Personally, I use a three-part, factfinding approach. The first part covers vital statistics, the second part discusses family situations and the third addresses financial status.

Oscar Mink is with Olympus Planning & Benefits in Lake Arrowhead, Calif. Mink is a Court of the Table qualifier and specializes in estate planning, life insurance and index annuities.

Once they "speak" it, repeat it.

You won't learn much about a prospect until you give him the opportunity to speak. The trick is to know the types of questions to ask to let a prospect open up. The question, "Are you comfortable with your current estate plan?" may sound insightful when you ask it, but it only requires the respondent to give you a one-word response. "What is your single greatest concern about your estate if you die?" is a good example of an open-ended question. It's true that some prospects will still guard their answers, but others don't need much prodding to go off on a 20-minute spiel of taxes, market returns and what they really think of their son's wife.

Anybody can be trained to ask these good questions, but few advisors are interested in the answer or truly know what they're supposed to be hearing. By dropping a well-placed, open-ended question into a factfinding conversation, you will likely learn your prospect's greatest fear within seconds of asking the question. It's usually the first answer out of his mouth. It may be more emotional than practical, but you certainly can't ignore a statement like: "I certainly don't want my money going to the IRS!"

Quite the opposite. A good advisor will pick up on this emotional plea early and use it repeatedly during subsequent conversations to help close the deal. He will say: "I'm recommending this annuity because I know you don't want to pay taxes," or "I can recommend a plan that will protect your money from Uncle Sam." Those are comments that will get you and your prospect on the same page quickly.

Oscar Mink is with Olympus Planning & Benefits in Lake Arrowhead, Calif. Mink is a Court of the Table qualifier and specializes in estate planning, life insurance and index annuities.

Forms or no forms?

This requires some instinct on your part, but it's possible to win or lose a client the moment you pull out your factfinder sheet. I have found that older, wealthier clients are more impressed with me if I'm armed with nothing more than a blank notepad. A prospect like this is interviewing me as much as I'm interviewing him, and a factfinder may seem like a crutch for the conversation or may not make me appear confident.

On the other hand, younger clients may demand forms. They want to know that I have a good support system behind me if I'm going to help manage their money. They may see a blank notepad as completely unprofessional and lose confidence in my abilities before I even get a chance to show them what I can do.

Oscar Mink is with Olympus Planning & Benefits in Lake Arrowhead, Calif. Mink is a Court of the Table qualifier and specializes in estate planning, life insurance and index annuities.

Send spouses to separate corners.

Because we work primarily with couples, we recognize the value in getting them to work as a team during the planning process. To achieve this client unity, near the beginning of the factfinding process, we ask each spouse to fill out the same 39-question form. We don't ask accounting-type questions, but we ask questions that are more along the lines of how they acquired their wealth, to whom they feel obligated for this wealth, their financial-independence dreams, as well as a list of planning affirmations to achieve their dreams. The differing results are pretty amazing.

Every relationship has points of contention that, for better or worse, go unresolved. But when it comes to financial planning, spouses need to agree before we can go any further into the planning process. We tell the couples prior to completing these forms that they're going to be edified and surprised by their answers.

We don't pressure them by making them fill out the questionnaires in our office, either. The couple is free to complete the questionnaire at home and mail it back to us. It only takes 30 minutes for them to fill out, but the conflicts we can nip in the bud using this process make this an invaluable factfinding tool.

Chris Jacob is with Michaletz & Jacob Wealth Advisory Group in St. Louis, Mo. Jacob and his partner Joe Michaletz are Top of the Table qualifiers who specialize in IRA planning and estate protection. They use the Legacy Wealth Optimization System to aid their factfinding process.

Don't short the factfinding process.

Is one hour enough time to recommend a product or a plan to a prospect? How about two? In our case, 30 hours of factfinding is what we need to become a prospect's most valued advisor. Our first meeting alone may take 90 minutes; we follow that up with a discovery meeting that explores the questionnaires we ask our prospects to complete.

If, after these two meetings, we've determined that we should proceed with a prospect, we will host a taped "biography" session that can last upwards of four hours. We ask questions about where the prospect grew up, where he went to grade school and all the way up to the present. (It's amazing what you miss in a conversation after you read a transcription.) From that point, we incorporate this biography into the existing information to create a family philosophy. Then we go to the numbers and delve into the prospect's financial fears.

From the time we first meet a prospect to when we finally recommend a financial plan for him, we may have put in a week's worth of work before anybody writes us a check. Visiting a financial advisor isn't like going to a doctor where he can pinpoint a patient's ailments in one visit. Besides, if a prospect is willing to come on this factfinding journey with us, he is going to feel more confident letting us handle his money than any other financial advisor he may currently retain.

Developing this exclusive bond is why we spend so much time getting to know our clients.

Chris Jacob is with Michaletz & Jacob Wealth Advisory Group in St. Louis, Mo. Jacob and his partner Joe Michaletz are Top of the Table qualifiers who specialize in IRA planning and estate protection. They use the Legacy Wealth Optimization System to aid their factfinding process.

My office is better than their office.

I prefer to hold 90 percent of my factfinders in my office, even if it means having to delay a meeting for a month. Because I work with successful business owners and other professional types, I feel that it's easier for the client to focus on what we're trying to accomplish.

At my office, the phone, a coworker or a computer can't distract the prospect. Holding the factfinder at my office also builds my credibility with the prospect. Until that meeting, he only knows me via the phone or through a visit to his office. By coming to my office, the prospect knows that I'm not operating out of the back of a truck.

Danny Moore, CSA, an MDRT qualifier, is with Moore Financial Management in Overland Park, Kan. He specializes in annuities, life insurance and personal lines for small-business owners. You may reach him at 913-681-1270.

Different strokes for different folks.

I didn't realize this until recently, but 75 percent of all my clients are women (not bad for a big ugly guy). I've learned that a woman's age and career status can tip you off about how to run your factfinding session with her.

Older women, the group I call the G.I. generation because they ran the house during the wars, need a lot of time. They like to talk about themselves and the history leading to the present. Even when you recommend a product to them, they want to know everything about that product and why you recommended that instead of another product. They like everything in writing. Maybe it's because they believe they have earned the right to speak at length, but you have to become a patient listener.

Baby Boomer women, on the other hand, don't have enough time. They're fast trackers who, to paraphrase Dwight Eisenhower, want everything on one page. In other words, they want to know what they can expect from the meeting and want to know everything about me in the shortest time possible. Baby Boomer prospects will likely have a finite amount of time with you; yet they expect you to treat them as if they are your only clients.

Generation X women don't care about glass ceilings and expect to be treated honestly. They can see through fluff, and if you don't follow through with them once, you're gone.

Danny Moore, CSA, an MDRT qualifier, is with Moore Financial Management in Overland Park, Kan. He specializes in annuities, life insurance and personal lines for small-business owners. You may reach him at 913-681-1270.

Tap into your prospect's personality.

If you're going to sell what the prospect wants to buy, you have to see the world through the prospect and find out what makes him tick rather than what you think he ought to have. I'm a big believer in social styles. I break everyone down into four categories: expressive, amiable, analytical and driver. I try to figure out which style they fit by starting the interview with an oddball question such as, "What would you want to give to your family if this were your last day on earth?"

Amiables will talk ad nauseum, analyticals will go home and type out your answers for you but expressives and drivers are harder to crack. Expressives want to be praised for their actions while drivers won't give you the time of day unless there's value in the exercise for them.

You don't need to change to the different personalities when marketing to these folks; it's just easier to work with them after you've pinpointed their social style.

Danny Moore, CSA, an MDRT qualifier, is with Moore Financial Management in Overland Park, Kan. He specializes in annuities, life insurance and personal lines for small-business owners. You may reach him at 913-681-1270.

Take time to document your factfinding meetings properly.

Clients are slowly beginning to realize that they can do most of their financial planning in one fell swoop. No longer do they have to visit different financial planners for their different financial needs. As a result, I believe that if you don't have control of all of your client's assets, you run the risk of letting those outside advisors come in and wrest control of what you've worked so hard to build. The foundation of all of this comes from documenting your client's concerns and dreams during the factfinding deliberations.

What's the best way to remember everything your prospects and clients say? Include a secretary or junior associate in the meeting to take complete notes while you chat with the client, eye to eye. The ideal situation is to have the associate or secretary out of your client's view so that both of you can chat freely. If you are forced to take notes during the meeting, you will spend half your time with your head down and you will never get a feel for your client's body language as he describes his most important concerns.

Of course, not many advisors have the luxury of having a secretary to take notes at the drop of a hat; so a viable option may be the use of a tape recorder. While a tape recorder is very accurate and doesn't miss a word, I've found that some clients can be intimidated by it and aren't as comfortable discussing concerns with me.

To cover our bases, we take notes from the factfinding meeting and condense them into the plan we recommend for the client. If the client agrees to our strategy, he will sign that written plan, which becomes the official documentation for that case.

Dennis Holmstrom is with Sjoberg Holmstrom LLC in
Mora, Minn. You may reach him at 320-679-5183 or at
Sjobergholmstrom@aol.com.

PRESENTATION

Lean back when appropriate.

When a high-toned, energetic communication with a client is not working, try leaning back.

For most successful advisors, leaning back is counter-intuitive. After all, in large part, their success came from their ability to push through, their energy, their drive, etc. As valuable as these attributes are, there are times when the opposite—the ability to lean back, get "lighter" and let the client come to you—is just as important.

Leaning back is not about taking it easy or succumbing to failure. It is not kicking back. It is about giving the client a chance to come to you. This is a fully intentional shift from pushing through to the client to enticing him to come your way.

This skill is especially important when times are tough and clients are scared. Pushing rarely works; yet, that is what most financial advisors instinctively do because they don't know any other way.

Leaning back starts with your attitude and extends to your body posture and words. Needy people lean forward, talk more loudly and push. Confident people lean back, talk more softly and draw others in.

The next time your client presentation is not working, don't lean forward and get louder. Force yourself to lean back and talk more softly. Do it with confidence and a firm intention to succeed.

Alan J. Parisse of the Parisse Group, Inc., can be contacted at 1630 30th Street—PMB# 310, Boulder, CO 80301. His phone number is 303-444-8080.

Get the client to think "bigger."

Whenever I sell insurance, I always talk about waiver of premium and double indemnity. Double indemnity has always bothered me. Why should you get paid double if you die accidentally?

So I say to the customer, "If you really need double the insurance, why not take a term rider instead of just the accidental policy? You'll find the cost is not that much greater."

For example, if you have $100,000 of whole life and you think you'll need $200,000 if you die unexpectedly, why not add a term rider for the extra $100,000 for 10 years? The advantage is that in case of death by sickness, the beneficiary gets the double benefit. After five or six years, you can convert that term rider. You can't convert double indemnity.

Why not sell a $200,000 policy to begin with? Well, that's the point. Giving the client an alternative to the double indemnity gets him to think "bigger."

Bill Lichtenstein, CLU, is with New York Life in Deerfield, Ill. He can be contacted at 847-317-8741 or wlz@ft.newyorklife.com.

Ditch the pitch.

Ask most people how they would describe a good salesperson, and they're likely to respond: "a good talker."

Talking, however, is probably the least important of all the attributes of sales success. Addressing the unique concerns of an individual or a specific group cannot and will not happen if you go into the close armed with all of the reasons why your company's 401(k) plan is designed to fit all the buyer's needs. It will not happen if you expect them to listen to a monologue that is all about you. It will not happen if you fail to respect their schedules and if you exceed the time they've been kind enough to give you.

It can happen

It can and *will happen*, however, if you revert to one of the fundamentals of Sales School 101: Your potential client wants to know: "What's in it for me?" To answer that question, you must ask what's important to him, listen closely and respond in a way that removes any obstacles or objections. To get started, heed some simple advice:

- Bring your presentation or PowerPoint slides that address all the benefits and advantages of your company's plan. Just don't open with the presentation.

- Bring a flip chart and several markers, and make sure the room is organized in a useful way. Position the flip chart prominently in front of your audience.

- Make the necessary introductions and then surprise your audience by shifting the focus on them.

A different start

Rather than launching into your sales pitch, you may want to begin with something like this:

"Tom, Dave and Mary, thank you very much for taking the time to meet with me today. I have reviewed your request for proposal and have a good general sense of what you're looking for in a 401(k) plan and program provider.

"However, what I would like to know from each of you is, given your different roles in the organization, what is your idea of the perfect plan? What is the most important thing you want to accomplish in choosing a program provider?"

Once their shock wears off, spend a moment or two with each person. Using your flip chart, write down their concerns: service, cost, flexibility, statements, etc. This creates a working document that everyone in the room will refer to as a list of the meeting's key objectives.

If your audience doesn't immediately open up, you may want to draw on the RFP to create leading questions. For example, you can say: "Mary, I understand that employee education is a top priority, but the workers on the third shift often miss the enrollment meetings. Is that correct? OK, so let's put 'education for all employees' on the board."

You also may want to review what you've heard them say. "Thank you, Tom, Dave and Mary, for your feedback. Just to recap: In addition to the objectives outlined in the RFP, the most important issues for us to address today are service, cost, flexibility…"

Ready to go

Now you may begin your presentation. It is not very important that the flow of your slides mirrors the list on your flip chart. It is important that you address their concerns thoroughly, confidently and in a manner that demonstrates what's in it for each of them. Cross off each item on the list after you and your audience are satisfied. Be sure to illustrate how every feature of the plan you're selling is a benefit that addresses their needs.

Once your presentation is complete, immediately draw their attention back to their list of objectives. Ask them if there are other questions that should be answered. If there are, answer them. It's at this point that a piece of psychology is often introduced into the sales equation: The psychology of the closer.

Though you may have removed all obstacles and objections to the close during your presentation, all your efforts will be in vain if you get tangled up in the fear of immediate rejection and neglect to ask for the business. If you hear "no" or something like it, don't panic. Ask why, address the concern and ask for the business again.

In some cases, the audience before you may not be authorized to make a decision. Don't get complacent if that happens. Confirm that all of their concerns have been addressed and there are no lingering obstacles to their recommending your company to be their 401(k) program provider. Once you've received that confirmation, you can walk away feeling good that you've done your job.

It's not over, though. Follow up promptly, restate how you will address their concerns, ask for the business and anticipate a "yes."

E. Thomas Foster Jr., Esq., is Hartford Life's 401(k) national key account manager and corporate spokesperson. He has 27 years of experience working with defined-contribution retirement plans. He may be reached at thomas. foster@hartfordlife.com.

CLOSE

Give prospects time to talk it over.

If you are having a consultation with more than one prospect, they have a tendency to want to discuss issues privately before making a decision to purchase whatever you are selling. However, once they walk out of your office, your chances of closing the sale decrease dramatically. You'll still close some of them, but even with those, you'll spend a good deal of time and effort chasing the prospects down and getting them back into the office.

Rather than letting them go home to "think about it," tell them you have to make a couple of phone calls, and that you'll leave them alone for a bit to talk it over. You will return in a while to hear their decision. You'll greatly increase your closing rate.

Mark Merenda, president of Smart Marketing, provides marketing consulting services to financial planning professionals. Contact him at 239-403-7755 or www.smartmarketingnow.com.

Ask your prospects to commit.

An effective closing technique is to get your prospects to commit, at the beginning of a consultation, to making a decision at the end of the meeting. This technique, sometimes called the "relationship close," goes something like this: "Now Mr. and Mrs. Jones, I'm happy to meet with you today and to give you my full attention and my best advice during this consultation. Because I'm doing this free of charge, I ask for only one thing: At the end of the hour, you tell me either yes or no. If the answer is yes, we'll be delighted. If the answer is no, we'll still part as friends. Do you think you can do that? Can you look me in the eye and tell me 'no' if that is your decision?"

Almost always, the prospect will agree that he can tell you "no." Now you have the prospect committed to a decision, and you've taken "I'll think about it" out of play.

Mark Merenda, president of Smart Marketing, provides marketing consulting services to financial planning professionals. Contact him at 239-403-7755 or www.smartmarketingnow.com.

Develop a credible relationship with your prospect if you want to close a sale.

Suppose you want to book a trip somewhere. What is your first step? No doubt, like millions of others you log onto the Internet and browse travel sites to compare prices.

What does this have to do with closing a sale? It means that the Information Age, which makes your life as a consumer easier, poses a threat to your life as a salesperson. Consumers armed with an Internet connection are just clicks away from all kinds of price and product comparisons. Your role as a salesperson is changing as a result.

Credibility is key

Making sales in such a price-savvy market can be tough for many sales professionals. To successfully transition to this I-can-get-prices-on-my-own environment, sales professionals must be able to put themselves in the role of making credible recommendations on what their clients should buy.

Fortunately, insurance and financial products are considered by most consumers and businesses to be complex purchases. Although consumers can access pricing, they often cannot get a detailed explanation of how products work, which they need to make the right purchase. Information overload can then occur, leaving consumers confused. This confusion creates an opportunity for you to help clients sort things out and make those credible recommendations.

It's not what you say

Product knowledge alone, however, doesn't develop credibility. Credibility comes with relationships. A relationship is the magic oil that turns the factual information and product knowledge into a trustworthy plan that your clients and prospects will buy.

According to research gathered by the Gallup Organization, it's not how you say something that makes someone believe you; it's how that person feels about you. Consider this example: A sales manager recounted the first time he observed one of the best sales agents in his company. "Tom had a reputation for producing exceptional results year after year, so I was really looking forward to hearing his presentations. On the very first presentation, though, I thought I was being set up for a practical joke. I had never heard anyone give such a clumsy presentation. I was tempted to silence Tom and continue the presentation myself. Much to my surprise, as Tom concluded his rambling explanation, the customer shook her head and agreed to buy."

The manager quickly realized that Tom's customers did not mind his clumsy presentations at all. Why? Because Tom was able to develop an important relationship with them—a relationship based on trust. His "nonslick" presentations worked to his advantage; the customer did not feel intimidated.

The right ingredients

Consumers today are also weary of salespeople trying to pull the wool over their eyes. Therefore, to make the sale, you must pay as much attention to the kind of relationship you are building with your customer as to the information you are providing. Give your clients and prospects only information that is relevant to their needs. Their ability to accept information from you will depend on their relationship with you. The right combination of information and relationship primes the pump for a purchase.

What are your relationship talents?

With what customers have you been able to establish your best relationships? What's the strongest characteristic that you have that makes people want to do business with you personally? What characteristics would you advertise about yourself? When you have thoroughly considered and answered these questions, you will have recognized what we call your "relationship talents."

In great salespeople, relationship talents—what will draw clients and prospects to them—are manifested in several ways. You may have exceptional empathy. You may be a great communicator. You may be openly friendly. You may find it easy to get another person to talk about himself. You may like to include people, to make them feel part of the group. Using these natural capabilities to cultivate a relationship instead of mimicking someone else will make you a great salesperson.

Gallup research showed us how one sales agent derived much of his success from his genuine "likeability." People quickly warmed up to him and viewed him as a welcome guest in person and on the phone. Another agent built trust through his dependability. These are two very different styles that worked equally well for two very different salespeople. Learn from these examples and use only those techniques that are a natural extension of your innate relationship talents.

Credible relationships: priceless

Your ability to form a productive relationship is crucial to your success. Extensive research shows that in developing a loyal customer, people are four times more important than the product or service itself—and 12 times more important than price alone.

The value of forming credible relationships with your customers is priceless. Credible relationships will close sales.

Benson Smith, an expert in sales effectiveness, is a speaker, author and consultant for the Gallup Organization. He is co-author of Discover Your Sales Strengths. *Jordan Missroon is a marketing and sales specialist. They may be reached at* benson_smith@gallup.com.

Ask prospects to insure the golden goose.

It is ironic that clients have no difficulty understanding the need to insure their property while ignoring the risks created by death or disability. This is why it is critical that we, as professional planners, possess the skills to help people understand that the greatest asset we have is our ability to go to work and earn an income. I have used the following presentation to help people understand the need to purchase disability income (DI) insurance:

"Let's talk about the problems of being disabled. Today you're healthy, you're working and you're earning. Those earnings support your lifestyle. An accident or illness can strike anytime. If the event disables you, you won't be working and you won't be earning. This will happen before age 55 to 25 percent of people your age. (See Table)

"The question is: How can we replace lost earnings? There are only three ways: The first is by invading our savings and investments. But even if we have set aside 10 percent of our income each year, one year of disability could wipe out 10 years of savings.

"The second option is to borrow. But without income will anyone lend us money? And even if they do, the loan plus the interest will have to be repaid.

"A third option is to insure the loss. This is accomplished by the purchase of a disability income policy which ensures a continuing flow of tax-free income at the precise moment we need it most."

I follow this presentation with a DI need analysis. The analysis compares existing income sources to the need for continuing income. I also point out that benefits from employer-paid coverage are taxable when received, and that 56 percent of all Social Security disability claims are rejected.

As part of my close I ask, "If you had a goose that was laying golden eggs, would you insure the goose or the eggs?" Unfortunately, most people insure the eggs. Perhaps it's time for us to insure the goose!

What are the chances of at least one 90-day disability before age 65?

Present Age	Probability
25	35%
35	31%
45	27%
55	23%

Thomas John Wolff, CLU, ChFC, served as 1979-1980 president of NALU (NAIFA). A member of MDRT since 1958, he is a recipient of the John Newton Russell Award. He is a member of Hartford AIFA (Conn.). His address is PO Box H, Vernon, CT 06066. You may reach him at 860-875-2591.

Give your prospects choices.

During evening dinner when my son was 6 years old, he steadfastly resisted eating the chili placed before him. Repeated requests that he do so were to no avail. Trying to get him to accept his fork had no effect. In a rare moment of brilliance, I asked him if he would use a fork or a spoon. He selected one and proceeded to finish his meal.

The moral of this story: Always give your prospect two "yes" options instead of "yes" or "no" options. That's the "chili" close!

Edward C. Auble, CLU, ChFC, MSFS, FLMI, LUTCF, of Paoli, Pa., can be contacted at 610-889-1640 or edauble@aol.com.

Learn what makes a "superior ask."

A healthy combination of information and relationship building merely primes the pump for customers to make a buying decision. More is usually required to turn your prospects' willingness into a signed contract. That "more" must come from you in the form of asking repeatedly and effectively.

What makes a "superior ask?" That depends on you. To be an effective closer, you must align your closing style with your underlying talents. Impacting talents are the ingrained aspects of an individual's personality that enable him to ask for, and gain, commitments from others. Here is a list of descriptions of the common impacting talents that we have found in great salespeople. Select the talent that best describes you.

The ability to command (COMMAND)

If you are a salesperson who has the talent to command, you like being in charge and in control of the conversation. You are quite adept at using questions to move people to make a commitment. You are not frightened by confrontation; rather, you know that confrontation is the first step toward resolution and that an initial "no" can often turn into a "yes."

The ability to develop (DEVELOPER)

You see the potential for success that exists for your clients. Your goal is to help your customers achieve that success. When you see a good match between your customers' needs and the products or services you offer, you are reluctant to let go. Your genuine interest in others often sways customers to follow your recommendations. You are willing to reassure your customers that you'll be there if something goes wrong.

The ability to maximize (MAXIMIZER)

You are excited about excellence and are at your best when calling on customers who have a similar drive to be the best. You become frustrated with individuals who only want to improve a little or may be satisfied with the status quo. Your customers are persuaded by the high-performance standards you set for yourself. You are willing to dare others to be great.

The ability to demonstrate a positive attitude (POSITIVELY)

As an advisor with the talent to be positive, you have a contagious enthusiasm and see the glass as half-full. You are generous with praise and quick to smile. No matter how serious the moment, you are able to keep your perspective. This quality makes others respond favorably as you implore them to "just do it." You know that people often need to be nudged into action and can usually sense when people's resistance is melting away.

The ability to believe (BELIEF)

You would never recommend a product unless you really felt it was in the customer's best interest. Ethics and responsibility are important to you. These qualities come across to your customers and help build trust. Your strong sense of belief will enable you to keep on asking for the sale even in the face of resistance. Your absolute conviction helps sway others to your point of view.

After you select the one talent that best describes you, start to build a closing style around it. The talents identified above are like muscles. They develop a memory of their own, and the more you use them, the stronger they become. Also, each time you experience success with a customer, analyze how your impacting talent helped to achieve that success. This will embolden you to rely on it more and to ask questions frequently and effectively.

Making a sale is very much about asking for the business. Our research shows that once you find the best way to impact others, you will experience a heightened sense of enjoyment in your job, greater customer loyalty and improved productivity.

Benson Smith and Tony Rutigliano are Gallup's leading experts in the area of sales force effectiveness. They may be reached at benson_smith@gallup.com.

What if...?

A client developed a new manufacturing process. One person in his organization was the genius behind the idea. I had unsuccessfully tried to sell keyperson insurance on that individual. One day I walked into the client's office, picked up the phone and said, "Gene, if this phone rang right now and the voice at the other end said, 'Don was killed in an auto accident,' what would you do?"

Gene was stunned. He said nothing. Finally, he responded, "How much did you say that policy cost?"

He wrote a check that morning.

Thomas John Wolff, CLU, ChFC, served as 1979-1980 president of NALU (NAIFA). A member of MDRT since 1958, he is a recipient of the John Newton Russell Award. He is a member of Hartford AIFA (Conn.). His address is PO Box H, Vernon, CT 06066. You may reach him at 860-875-2591.

Use the following classic sales closes.

The Ben Franklin close: Draw a line down the center of a sheet of paper and say: "Bill, let us list those features you like the best about this plan and the features you like the least."

The relevant-story close: "Bill, as we were talking, I was reminded of one client who purchased a plan but who died in an auto accident before his policy came back for delivery. Fortunately, he did not put off buying the policy. Did you know that every 14 minutes, someone buys life insurance but does not live long enough to pay the second premium?"

The please-forgive-me close: "By the way, before I go, I know you are not purchasing a plan today, but I was wondering if you could help me with my presentation. Would you tell me the real reason why you are not going with me on this?"

The final-alternative close: "Would you prefer the premium to be drafted from your bank account each month on the first or the 15th?"

The ultimatum close: "Bill, you know that we have discussed this quite a bit. I realize this is taking a lot of your time, so this is either a good idea or it is not. Let us make a decision right now."

The decision close: "I am not going to try to sell you anything. I am just going to show you some reasons other people have purchased this plan."

John W. French Sr. of Austin, Texas, can be contacted at 512-219-4077 or at jwfrenchins@yahoo.com.

REFERRALS

To encourage referrals, give blank phone directories to clients and prospects.

Buy some blank phone directories with alphabetical tabs. These can be fancy desktop types that cost $20 or more, or the pocket sort produced by sales promotional firms that cost less than a dollar. The cost is not the object.

When you visit your clients and centers of influence, hand them a phone directory. Resist the "put it in the mail" method of delivery—it doesn't work. When you are face to face with your client, say something like this: "Because you are my valued client, I brought you this phone directory. So you can always find me, I have already put my name here under 'N' for Ned, under 'R' for Ricks, under 'I' for insurance and also under the name of my company."

After your client thanks you, ask him: "Who else would be among the first people you want to put in your new phone book?" These are usually the most important people to the client. Ask if you may call on them to make their acquaintance so that when they need an insurance professional, you will already be in their phone book.

Ned B. Ricks, CLU, is managing member of Guidon Consulting, of Gurnee, Ill. Contact him at 847-856-8826 or NedR0003@aol.com.

Create a referred-lead program that works.

The following describes a process that has produced high-quality referrals for us. This process begins with mailing a letter to people we know, regardless of whether or not they have done business with us. The common factor here is that they know us, and there is a level of confidence and trust. Following is a sample request-for-referrals letter.

A form (see Sample A) is mailed with this request-for-referrals letter. Once our client completes the form, he mails it back in a return envelope.

Upon receipt, we mail an approach letter to the referred leads we have received. We usually accompany this piece with a press kit, which tells the prospect what we do. This takes the form of either an audiocassette tape or a brochure, which includes our picture.

After no more than a week, we follow up with a phone call to the referred lead to request an appointment. I have found that unless there is a system in place, the referred-lead question is often overlooked during the interview with a client. Our system enables us to ask for referrals several times a year and to ask for them not just from people with whom we have done business, but from those who are already familiar with us and feel comfortable in referring us to other clients.

In closing: Don't expect to get referred leads unless you also give referred leads.

Request-for-referrals letter

Date
James Smith
123 Main Street
Anywhere, NY 10001

Dear James,

It has been 15 years since I started building an organization involved in the insurance planning industry. Our knowledge, experience and manpower have earned us a reputation as a service organization that is dedicated to providing insurance and financial programs for individuals and businesses.

I am writing to ask for your help in introducing me to people like you who might need someone to help analyze their financial and insurance goals and develop plans to reach those goals. As I'm sure you can understand, almost everyone is more comfortable working with someone who is referred to her than working with a stranger.

Our process of developing a relationship consists of two stages. The first requires you to complete the enclosed form, titled, "Do You Know Someone Who ...?" [See Sample A.] This form helps bring to mind people you know who are in situations that usually require financial and insurance planning. The second stage happens after we receive this form back from you. We then send a letter with a reply slip and a self-addressed, stamped return envelope to the people from your list. This letter asks them to return the reply slip if they are interested in receiving more information about financial and insurance plans.

Please realize that my approach involves service before sales, without any degree of pressure to buy. Any plans that are created have been developed from my client's goals.

Please return the enclosed form if you know of someone whose circumstances warrant the services of my organization or if I can be of help to you.

Thank you.

Sample Form "A"
Do You Know Someone Who ... (Please give their name, address and phone number.)

- *Recently started her first job or was promoted?*

- *Was just married or has become engaged?*

- *Has a new baby or is expecting?*

- *Has young children who may someday go to college?*

- *Recently bought a home?*

- *Moved here from out of town?*

- *Is a partner or an employee-stockholder in a business?*

- *Has just retired after a successful career?*

- *Has inherited money?*

- *Is especially interested in a particular charity?*

Jeffrey T. Wilkie, LUTCF, has been an agent and registered representative in the insurance and investment-planning arena for the past 16 years. Contact him at 888-616-5656.

Qualify referrals.

I deal in the family market. When delivering each policy, I ask for a copy of the will to confirm that the beneficiary designations are in harmony with the wishes expressed in the will. After getting the client to agree that nothing is more important than choosing the proper guardian for his minor children, I ask for referrals this way: "May I explain the honor and responsibility of being named guardian to each of your guardians and confirm that their wills and insurance policies are up to date?" I then get every detail possible to qualify those referrals.

Howard R. Utz is with Kansas City Life in Mars, Pa. You may reach him at 724-625-2099 or kclins1@nauticom. net.

"I love referrals."

Diana Borroel, a top producer with New York Life, is known as "The Lady Who Loves Referrals." Borroel has achieved Top Producer status with two simple strategies: She makes sure she does a great job for her clients, so she's referable quickly, and she constantly reminds her clients that she likes referrals.

Her business cards have the words "I love referrals" printed on them. Her notes to clients always end with: "I love referrals." And she always tells people: "I love referrals."

She also uses an audio business card that's called "Referring to You." And she's comfortable bringing up referrals and does it all the time.

Borroel's results have been nothing short of fantastic. Her style may or may not suit every advisor's style, but it doesn't matter. Just find a way to bring up referrals early and often without becoming pushy or obnoxious.

Bill Cates of Referral Coach International can be reached at 2915 Fenimore Road, Silver Spring, MD 20902, 301-949-6789, or at BillCates@ReferralCoach.com.

Ask for referrals in a client-centered way.

A client-centered approach to referrals always puts the client's or prospect's interests first. For example, if you want to tell people you get paid with referrals, make sure you do it in a client-centered manner.

"The second way I get paid is that if you see the value in the work I do for you, you'll introduce me to others who might also value this work. What this means to you is: I hope to earn the right to those referrals. I'll make sure you get the perfect policy. I'll make sure you understand everything along the way. If any problems arise, I won't run away. I'll be there for you. Because of my value and service, I hope you'll feel comfortable in introducing me to your friends and associates."

The key phrase here is what this means to you. Whenever you tell people about your practice, if you're saying "what this means to you" and following this up with a benefit to those people, you're being client-centered.

Bill Cates of Referral Coach International can be reached at 2915 Fenimore Road, Silver Spring, MD 20902, 301-949-6789, or at BillCates@ReferralCoach.com.

Use these questions to find out more about people who were referred to you.

- Why did you think of him first?

- Has he expressed a concern in this area?

- Could you give me a sense of his personality?

- How do you think he'll react to his name coming up in conversation and my calling him?

- What do you think is the best way to approach him, so that he'll be open to speaking with me?

- Could you tell me something that you like or admire about him?

I need to emphasize the importance and power of that last question. Every time you get a referral, ask your source what he admires about his friend. Then use this in your opening conversation with your prospect.

Bill Cates of Referral Coach International can be reached at 2915 Fenimore Road, Silver Spring, MD 20902, 301-949-6789, or at BillCates@ReferralCoach.com.

Learn how to use referrals.

There will be times when you ask for referrals and your referral source gets into what I call a "stream of consciousness." He'll rattle off a dozen names or more. Sometimes, he'll grab his business or association directory and feed you a ton of names. When you catch your client doing this, don't stop him. Write the names down and encourage him to give you more names.

After the flood is over, identify three to five people you want to learn more about, so you can have a high-quality conversation with them. Tell your referral source you've learned through experience that you'll be more successful in reaching and helping these people if you take a few at a time and learn as much as you can about them. Then tell your referral source you'll call him in a week to learn more about the next "batch."

Bill Cates of Referral Coach International can be reached at 2915 Fenimore Road, Silver Spring, MD 20902, 301-949-6789, or at BillCates@ReferralCoach.com.

Here are nine ways to boost referrals.

If you're like most insurance advisors, increasing your client base is your top priority. But cold calling is far from the best way to attract new clients. Referrals, on the other hand, are. Here are nine sure-fire ways to increase the number of referrals you receive from your clients:

1. Create an information folder.

Too many advisors view referrals as something extra—a bone a client tosses them every once in a while. You need to change this way of thinking. Everything you do should be geared toward asking for, and following up on referrals and that means creating a system. With a system in place, you won't have to think: "What should I send to this referral?" or "How should I thank this client for giving me this referral?" Instead, you should have readily available an introductory information folder about yourself and the services you provide, which you can easily drop in the mail. It should be as automatic as checking your email.

2. Give clients an experience.

To get referrals, you must make working with you a memorable, one-of-a-kind experience. Make your clients want to refer their friends to you. Develop a tagline that cleverly conveys who you are: "John Smith—Wealth Producer." But that's just the start of the experience. You need to take it further.

One financial services firm tells its clients it will help them "get to the top of the mountain." The top of the mountain suggests they can see all around the world. To emphasize that, the company has turned each of its offices and conference rooms into a different "country." One room has a large mural of Athens on the wall, another depicts Paris, and so on. The company says its clients often bring their friends by to see the offices, even without an appointment. Can you imagine a better way to attract new business?

3. Find your niche.

You can't be all things to all people. Take stock of your expertise, areas of interest and the insurance products you sell, and determine the type of specialist you want to be. It should feel natural, as if you were born to play the role. Then cultivate that niche. Here are some things you can do:

- Contact *Advisor Today* and offer to write a sales article.

- Become a prominent member of your local association.

- Hold insurance seminars and workshops for the public. This will establish you as an expert.

- Distribute testimonials and tell success stories about your practice.

4. Keep in touch.

Initiate regular contact with your clients; don't wait for them to call you. You should create a monthly contact system for communicating with your best clients. For example, in February, send a valentine; in June, offer helpful travel tips; in November, share a holiday recipe, and ask for theirs.

It's essential to contact special clients several times a year just to make sure they are happy with your service. But keeping in touch is more than an automatic mailing. It's a way of telling clients you are there to help them solve their financial problems.

5. Become a list lord.

An association or club list can help you get referrals. Suppose you're sitting across the table from someone who's a member of, for instance, the Springfield Country Club. Just pull out your list and say, "I was wondering if you know anyone in this club who might be interested in life insurance." This works because people like to show that they have influence in the groups to which they belong.

6. Use a RR crossing sign.

Put a big sign in your office that says "RR." To you, it means Remember Referrals, but it may also prompt visiting clients to ask what it means. This gives you the perfect opening to explain that referrals are the heart of your business and you would appreciate their help.

7. Start a referral club.

Start a referral club consisting of members of your local business community. The club creates a sense of camaraderie among your fellow businesspeople, and it's a forum for sharing referrals among members.

8. Say thank you.

Thanking clients who give you referrals encourages more referrals. You should reward these valuable clients with a nice letter or note. In addition, try sending them flowers or gift baskets. Here are a few other gift suggestions:

- A book on a subject they're interested in

- Homemade cookies or other treats

- Tickets to a sporting event, the theater or the movies

- A gift certificate to a spa

- A coupon for a free car wash or dry cleaning

9. Do it every day.

The best way to get comfortable with asking for referrals is to make it part of your everyday business dialogue. At the end of each appointment, ask your clients, "Is there anyone else you know who may need insurance?"

I cannot overstate the importance of asking for referrals. These leads are easy to close and usually turn out to be loyal customers.

Maribeth Kuzmeski is president and founder of the consulting firm Red Zone Marketing in Libertyville, Ill. She is also the author of the book, 85 Million Dollar Tips for Financial Advisors. *Contact her at* www.redzonemarketing.com *or* mk@redzonemarketing.com. *or 847-367-4066.*

Here are four ways to generate referrals.
1. Make yourself referable.
Do this by pointing out to clients the "impressive outcomes" you are achieving for them so they want to refer you, instead of you having to ask for a referral. Also, giving impeccable service to your clients helps make you more "referable."

2. Cultivate centers of influence.
Pursue referrals from professionals who comprise your clients' advisory teams, like estate-planning attorneys and accountants. Phoning them is the most direct way to get this relationship started.

3. Extend your network.
Ask clients who else they have working toward their financial well-being, and then let those professionals know exactly what you are doing for their client. If you are too busy to do this, outsource it.

4. Don't stop.
A referral system—of any kind—will not produce results unless you keep at it. And remember that when you do get a referral, a simple thank-you is invaluable.

(Reported in Advisor Today*)*

ACROSS THE BOARD

Cultivate the Wow! factor.

"Meet, exceed, wow!" is the motto of the Borislow Insurance Agency staff. The focus on cultivating the client relationship has led to an abundance of business activity and a bounty of referrals. "We set the clients' expectations and do everything possible to exceed them" explains Jennifer A. Borislow, with Borislow Insurance Agency, Inc. "Then we create the Wow! factor."

An example of the Wow! factor was the client who needed a new company health insurance plan within a week. Borislow pulled it off in two days: "The client said, 'Wow! I can't believe you've entered my life.' People are tired of bad service reps saying 'I can't do that.'"

With only 10 employees, the firm's small size allows it to have more contact with clients. It also spends a third of its budget on technology to keep track of important client data. The staff uses the data to help develop and build loyalty. It does it with techniques such as recognizing special events in the client's life—from birthdays to the anniversary of the death of a loved one—and getting involved in charitable and community events.

Then there is Borislow's special niche—a must in this competitive market. "You can't be a generalist and make it in the business," she emphasizes. She also points to the fact that her volume of work with insurance carriers guarantees a difference in rates and products, which gets passed on to clients.

Borislow says she has no trouble selling, and client meetings are key. There are important elements that she always takes with her to these meetings: a passion for her work and keen listening skills. Asking questions in a client meeting is critical: "The more questions you ask, the easier it is to close, as they've given you the answers to what's important to them," she says.

Borislow also never forgets the follow-up, including notes for her file on action items with target and completion dates. "How many times have you had a great meeting with a professional, but after that nothing happens?" she asks. "We make things happen."

(Reported by Lynn Vincent, contributor to Advisor Today)

Make your customer your advocate.

Our research shows that "customer engagement"—that rational and emotional attachment a customer has to you and your company—is the best measure of sales success. This attachment consists of the customer's satisfaction, his likelihood to purchase from you again and his willingness to be an advocate or referral.

How do you develop engaged customers? There is no magic bullet. Your own engagement level is the best explanation of your ability to develop customers who are advocates for you.

To enhance your level of engagement, you should ask yourself three questions: How clear are my expectations? Do I have the resources necessary to do the job? Do I do every day what it is I do best?

When sales representatives work for themselves, they frequently allow their expectations to become muddy. If you want to be successful, you should make it a point to set clear, short-term, measurable objectives. Prioritize those goals. What is it that you want to get done this month, this week or even today? Write your expectations down and be sure to discuss those objectives and priorities with your support staff. When you leave your office every day, you should have a good idea just how much you have accomplished. This sense of accomplishment directly translates into higher engagement levels—and to more sales.

Next, avoid skimping on resources in an effort to save money. As one manager aptly put it, "If your office is a dump, you'll inevitably end up feeling dumpy." While office decor or the latest electronic gadgets may not directly boost your productivity, they can improve the way you feel about yourself and your work. Invest in your own development as well. Books, magazine articles and seminars can spark your professional growth.

Finally, don't allow yourself to become bogged down with activities far removed from what you do best. If you do, you will be reducing the likelihood of developing engaged customers. You may be able to grind out transactions, but you will not be building a solid business base. Your customers may buy from you, at least for a while, but they will not become willing advocates for you.

Benson Smith and Tony Rutigliano are Gallup's leading experts in the area of sales force effectiveness. Contact them at benson_smith@gallup.com.

Use your voice mail to sell.
Even your voice mail can help you sell to prospects and clients. Let me tell you why that can be very important.

This is an age when the difference is you. Clients want to hear from someone who speaks clearly about the results they can expect and the benefits they can receive. That is the essence of good marketing: to be in front of people and to share with power, precision and confidence the desired results and benefits that you and your services can bring to them. Each day you are on the phone or away from your desk, that simple little voice mail can help remind people of the difference you can make in their lives, their families, their businesses and their future security.

Why not begin today to define the powerful benefits your focused practice brings to your clients and prospects? Start every day in a marketing mindset by using your voice mail to market yourself and sell your services. Use a benefits-based mission statement to make new and creative voice mail messages daily. These help attract and interest potential clients.

To do this, get to the office early and change your message to something like this: "Hello, this is (your name) of (your group). Today is (day and date)." Then, follow this with a short statement of the benefits your service offers people. Here are some examples to get you started:

- Today is Monday. We help people have better Mondays because they have a plan for the future. How can we help you?

- We help people make sure their retirement is safe and secure. How can we help you?

- We help people know that whatever happens to them, their family's future is secure. How can we help you?

- We help people disinherit the IRS. How can we help you?

- We help people pass on their faith and values to others. How can we help you?

- We help people make good choices to ensure that if they need long-term care, they, and not the government, get to choose that care. How can we help you?

- We help people work a plan to make sure their children can go to the college of their choice. How can we help you?

- We help people take the first step in planning for financial independence and true success. How can we help you?

- We help people become part of the successful few who are working a plan for financial independence and true success. How can we help you?

- We help people get started on investing in the stock market for just $50 a month. How can we help you?

These are just starters. You can create a message to suit your specific field. But, remember that whether or not you do a daily voice mail, the key is thoughtfulness. Every day, this exercise should cause you to think of how you want to bring results and benefits to your clients. This kind of thoughtfulness daily will help you deliver those results.

Stan Hustad heads the PTM Group, a performance coaching service based in Minneapolis. Contact him at ptmark@aol. com.

Run the bases.

Without knowing where you stand with a client, you can't employ the best strategy to move the sale forward. I refer to this as a baseball diamond—or knowing what base you're on.

Before hitting a home run (a sale), getting through the bases of the diamond is essential. You might move backward only to eventually move forward, closer to the closing technique you already use. Think of this as:

1st base—Chemistry: You have created a compatible chemistry through dialogue, investigation and mutual respect. You have established a certain amount of trust in the mind of your potential client. You share values in what's important to the buying-selling relationship, and both of you are on the same page of the client's needs and your solution.

2nd base—Needs expressed: You have created desire and need for more dialogue and the potential client expresses a need with you freely. He discovers where his individual pain points are, which you can use to learn and develop further. Is it safe to move forward to 3rd base?

3rd base—Value revealed: The potential client now expresses to you the value he will receive by moving forward in your process. He believes in you and sees benefits only you can deliver. His "generic" problem has become an individual personal problem, and you have discovered something about that problem that is important to you.

Knowing the emphasis and time you spend on each base determines how difficult or easy it will be to bring the decision "home" for a positive outcome or a sale. If you don't know what base you're on after using these criteria, and if you're searching for signals in the wrong area of the playing field, you'll miss the opportunity to move forward strategically to hit a home run.

Dick Zalack helps entrepreneurs develop personal strategic plans and small-business owners develop systems to hire, train and motivate staff. You may reach him at 330-225-0707 or www.focusfour.com.

Don't be a salesperson; be a trusted advisor.

Do you know what it's like when you nurture and cultivate a quality business relationship with clients? I mean when you've really done what it takes to earn their business, and they give you the chance you deserve? From then on, the floodgates for business, and referrals open up. If you have ever had the positive feelings that come with quality client relationships, then you have experienced the benefit of Influence Skill. By the same token, you may be experiencing some of the frustration that goes with a lack of Influence Skill.

Everyone has some level of Influence Skill, and all of us have untapped influence capacity. People with high levels of Influence Skill enjoy better quality relationships, longer-term relationships and substantially shorter sales cycles from the inception of the contact to the reality of, what I call, long-term, profitable business relationships.

So, what's the difference between persuasion techniques or closing tactics and Influence Skill? A persuasive person might convince a great white shark to become a vegetarian. No easy task! But a person of influence will create a situation in which the shark wants to become a vegetarian, is happy with the decision six months later, and actively refers other great whites to this person!

The power is not in the questions. The power is in the questioning process.

So what's the answer? What do you do, and how do you do it? Here are some areas to consider:

I believe Influence Skill is a "High TEQ" process. The T in the acronym stands for trust. The foundation for long-term, profitable business relationships is trust. Why do some people trust you and others do not? Have you really studied your quality relationships, looking for clues on how to improve all your business relationships? Even if you are good at establishing trust, how come it takes as long as it does to get trust and convert it into business? What would happen to your business if you could deliberately create trust in less time and on purpose, instead of by accident?

The E is for emotion. I can ask a room full of successful salespeople if people buy on logic or emotion and get a resounding "emotion." But if I ask that same room of successful salespeople to "emotion me," the room gets very quiet. Everybody knows people buy on emotion, so how come so few can create the emotions they want their prospects and clients to feel on purpose? Do you think in terms of the emotion you want to create and then deliberately create it, or do you fish for hot buttons and hope you catch the right one?

And the Q stands for questions. Influence is a function of trust. Trust is a function of understanding. Understanding is based on the quality of your questions and your ability to listen empathetically.

Dr. Stephen Covey, in his book 7 *Habits of Highly Effective People*, described empathic listening as "listening with the ears, eyes and heart—for feeling and meaning." Have you ever noticed how much more you trust people who really understand you? Top producers and people of influence ask questions to truly understand and empathize.

By mastering the ability to ask questions, learning to create appropriate emotional responses *on purpose*, and focusing on developing bonds of trust, you are well on your way to *values-based selling*. Don't delay. Start today by writing questions that create the emotional response you want, which causes your clients to buy from you the first time.

Don't be a salesperson; be a trusted advisor.

© 2003 by Bill Bachrach, Bachrach & Associates, Inc. All rights reserved. Bill Bachrach is the author of four industry-specific books, including It's All About Them; How Trusted Advisors Listen for Success. Contact him at 800-347-3707.

Want more appointments? Learn to say no.

Are you letting your prospects and clients limit the number of appointments you schedule each week? Let's suppose that you suggest to a prospect a meeting time of next Tuesday at 10 a.m. or Friday at 2:30 p.m. He says that next Tuesday will be fine, but can you make it at 11 a.m. instead? If you follow the plan I'm about to describe, the answer is NO. Here's why.

You have created an ideal work week schedule for yourself and have blocked off appropriate amounts of time for prospecting, phoning, appointments, paperwork, training and education, family time, etc. Using Tuesday as an example, let's assume you have blocked off the following times for appointments: 7 a.m., 8:30-9:30 a.m., 10-11 a.m., 11:30 a.m.-1 p.m., and 1:30-2:30 p.m. Five perfectly good appointment times. If you accommodate the prospect's request for an 11 a.m. appointment, you run the risk of converting two appointments (10-11 a.m. and 11:30 a.m.-1 p.m.) into just one appointment (11 a.m.-12 p.m.). This reduces the number of prospects or clients seen from five to four, a decrease of 20 percent. Assuming additional alterations are made to your schedule that week, you can potentially reduce the number of prospects or clients you can see that week by 30 percent, 40 percent or more. So be firm. Say no. Create an ideal schedule and stick to it to maximize your sales success.

Robert A. Arzt, CLU, ChFC, LLIF, is CEO of Polaris One. He coaches professionals who want to achieve more. Contact him at 301-610-5624, bob@bobarzt.com *or through his website at* www.PolarisOne.com.

Increase sales by decreasing clutter and stress.

Have you ever found a lead on a scrap of paper after the prospect purchased from your competition? Are you spending time recreating proposals because you can't find a similar one you wrote a few months ago? Do you run out the door for an appointment at the last minute because you couldn't find the brochures you really wanted to take? Are you feeling overwhelmed? If so, here are six steps to help you increase sales and decrease stress:

1. Make a date with yourself for getting your act together. Plan a minimum of three hours when there will be no interruptions. Decide on a reward for yourself when you're finished. Do anything you can to reduce your stress during the process—play music, grab your favorite beverage and get plenty of trash bags and recycling bins.

2. Take everything off your desk except what you must have or do. (A photograph or memento that reminds you of the reason you work is definitely OK.) Practice the art of wastebasketry. Research shows that 80 percent of what you keep you never use. Tossing or keeping is not a moral issue; it is a practical one. So how do you decide what to keep? Ask yourself: "What's the worst thing that could happen if I didn't have this piece of paper?" If you can live with the results of your answer, toss the piece of paper.

3. Get the right tools for your business. Half of any job is using the right tool. Put three trays on your desk labeled In, Out and File. "In" is for new mail—papers you have not yet looked at. "Out" is for items that need to go elsewhere, such as the post office or to another room. "File" is for papers you need to file outside the reach of where you sit. Eliminate paper whenever you can with electronic tools, such as a contact management program and a financial management program.

4. Implement The FAT System: File, Act or Toss. Clutter is postponed decisions. The good news? There are only three decisions you can make about what to do with any piece of paper. They are: File it in a reference file in case you need it in the future, Act on it immediately or in the near future, or Toss it.

5. Create an action filing system. Look at each piece of paper on your desk. Is the ball in your court to do this? That's an action file. Action files come in two varieties: (1) Temporary—These are tasks that have to be done once and will come to an end, such as an annual review. Sort these by date or by project name in your most accessible desk drawer. (2) Permanent—These are tasks you do over and over again, such as prospects to call, calls expected from prospects, PalmPilot entry, discuss with manager and expense reimbursements. Keep these in a file on top of your desk for a visual reminder.

6. Create a reference-filing system. If your existing filing system isn't working, start over. Keep the old papers, and as you need them, merge them into the new filing system. For electronic files, use a filing system program such as Taming the Paper Tiger. It creates and prints a file index as well as file labels and allows you to automatically cross reference files. With its powerful search engine capability, you can retrieve anything you file in five seconds by using a keyword search.

Will this system turn you into a perennially clean-desk person? Not likely. Messy desks are the natural outcome of a hectic pace. A place for everything and everything in its place—forget it. But it is half-right. A place for everything means that when you want to clean up your office to meet a client, or just because you're sick of the mess yourself, recovering is no big deal. Some quick decision making will clean your desk in a matter of minutes and bring back to you a sense of control.

© Barbara Hemphill 2003. Barbara Hemphill is CEO of Hemphill Productivity Institute, Raleigh, N.C. Contact her at 800-427-0237 or visit www.ProductiveEnvironment. com.

Remember: Selling is like playing billiards.

The sales game is much like billiards. In billiards, you're always looking several shots ahead. If you're trying to sink the six-ball, you want to do it in such a way as to put yourself in the perfect position to sink the three-ball on the following shot.

The same is true in sales. You want to make the sale with the existing prospect, but in a way that positions you to be introduced to others. Unlike billiards, where if you miss the six-ball, you lose your turn, in selling, you can still miss the sale, but get introduced to others—as long as you bring value to the game.

> *Bill Cates of Referral Coach International can be reached at 2915 Fenimore Road, Silver Spring, MD 20902, 301-949-6789, or at* BillCates@ReferralCoach.com.

Do not set sales goals.

Setting goals doesn't work. I've been at corporate retreats where companies roll out the annual sales goals only to watch the employees faint from apoplexy. Goals are pure fantasy unless you have a specific plan to achieve them. And, of course, nothing unexpected or weird gets in the way, like a war or a tornado that levels your plant. Simply announcing or wishing sales to be higher doesn't make it so. Worse, it may have the reverse effect if the team thinks the goal is unrealistic.

Sad to say, but without a disciplined roadmap, goals are worthless. You know why? Because writing down goals doesn't mean a thing until you realize that the goal is only the destination. How much thought have you given to the journey? Your answer should be "lots." You'll need to fill in a lot of holes between where you are now and where you want to go. A lot of work, huh? Well, each step has to be mapped out if you want to be able to check your position and stay on the right path.

Mapping also shows you how far you are from your goal and what part to do next.

That's exactly how writers work. They plot the course—step by tedious step. Novelists can't sit down and write 500 pages front to back. They outline. They put ideas on 3x5 cards and pin them all over the wall. Then, they move the cards around until the story makes sense. Usually, they sit down and write one chapter at a time, using cause and effect to make it intelligible. After a while, their collection of individual chapters equals one novel.

As a comedian, if my goal is to get a standing ovation, I have to carefully build each joke "hunk" to take the listener on a predetermined funny journey. The first five minutes are designed to introduce myself and give the audience a reason to stay invested in me for an hour. Then, I try a few comic premises and let the audience determine the subjects that interest them. In the final two minutes, I stack the jokes so that the laughs come every five seconds. Then, if I end with my strongest joke or story, I'll get my biggest, longest laugh. If I have done my job correctly, I'll build my act to end "on a roll." My success gauge is if the audience responds with 25 seconds of exit applause or if they come to their feet. It may sound like manipulation, but the audience gets what they want, and I accomplish my goal.

So the next time your boss gives you a sales goal, ask him/her how you all plan to get there. You can't just "voodoo" an increase of sales by 15 percent. There has to be a well thought out strategy. Strategy gives you confidence, direction, a measuring device and usually includes a Plan B. If he or she can't do that, then make it your goal to find another job.

Excerpted from the book Nobody Moved Your Cheese *by Ross Shafer, an Emmy-award-winning comedian, TV host and corporate motivational speaker. Visit* www.RossShafer. com.

Learn how to become a better and more active listener.

When you listen intently to what someone is telling you, you will have a very positive reaction when it is your turn to be heard. Unfortunately, salespeople seem to forget this all-important and commonly known fact when they try to convey the value of their products or services to their prospects and clients.

Actively listening to your prospect not only increases the effectiveness of the interaction; it also greatly increases your chance of making the sale. When you actively listen to the prospect, you are better able to understand that prospect's needs than when you don't give him your full attention. In turn, you are in a better position to express how your product or service can benefit him, his family or his business.

Here are 10 tips that can help you become a better and more active listener. If you pay attention and actively internalize these tips, you will be on your way to improving your sales skills and boosting your productivity.

1. Open your mind and ears.
You should switch off all negative thoughts and feelings about the person who is talking to you and be receptive to the messages he is giving. Don't allow your opinion of that person to interfere with your chances of eventually closing the sale. Perhaps you find how the person dresses or speaks to be distasteful. If you let this show, you may not get past the first few minutes of the conversation.

2. Listen from the first sentence.
You need to temporarily put aside or forget whatever it is that you're preoccupied with at the time of your interaction. If you appear preoccupied, then your prospect will know it and will surely feel unimportant. Trust me, any prospect who thinks he is unimportant to a salesperson will take his business elsewhere.

3. Analyze what is being said.

You shouldn't try to figure out or anticipate what the prospect will say to you. Rather, you should pay attention to exactly what he is saying at a given moment. Even the slowest listeners can think faster than the fastest talkers.

4. Really listen; don't just "not talk."

You should not only appear to be listening; you should also actively assist the prospect in conveying his message. If you do not give some sort of feedback to what your prospect is saying, he may feel you are not truly listening.

5. Never interrupt, but always be interruptible.

This is invaluable. Interrupting your prospect is not only rude; it will also greatly reduce your chances of making the sale. Conversely, if you allow the prospect to interrupt what you are saying, you appear to truly care about what he is saying. This will help build a very positive relationship.

6. Ask questions.

To stimulate people to talk and help you clarify your understanding of what they mean, let them know you are taking them seriously by drawing them out. When you ask questions, you reinforce the idea that you are truly listening, not simply standing there and waiting for your turn to speak.

7. Remember what is said.

This involves logging important points into your mental computer. You should take notes if necessary and try to make connections between apparently isolated remarks.

8. Block out interruptions and distractions.

This is an essential step in becoming an effective, active listener. You should concentrate so fully on what is being said that you don't notice visual or audible distractions. When you allow outside factors to steal your attention, your prospect may assume that your original attention was forced, dramatically decreasing your chances of completing a sale.

9. Be responsive.

This tip might not be obvious to some salespeople; in fact, many never seem to do it. You should get your whole body into listening and showing that you are paying attention. Look at the person squarely in the eyes and use facial expressions.

10. Stay cool.

This is the most important step in the process of active listening. You should be completely relaxed throughout the entire conversation with your client. Don't overreact to highly charged words and tones. Quite often, people calm down after they are allowed to vent their anger and frustration. Your calmness and relaxation will likely rub off on your prospect, creating an environment that is free of stress.

Enhance your chances.

Active listening is an important yet widely ignored aspect of selling. If you are unable to show your heartfelt interest in what your prospect is saying, you will greatly diminish your chances of actually closing the sale. On the other hand, if you use these tips to become an active listener, you are almost guaranteed to have many more productive and pleasant selling experiences.

Bill Brooks is CEO of The Brooks Group, an international sales training and business growth firm in Greensboro, N.C. For more information, visit www.brooksgroup.com *or call 336-282-6303.*

Here are some things you should stop doing right now.

Stop fooling yourself.

Those who try to con the customer only kid themselves. A phone call came from a telephone company representative who described a new approach to meeting the telecom needs of mid-sized businesses. To provide these services, the phone company was "partnering" with another firm to conduct a needs assessment and make recommendations.

When the report was presented several weeks later, potential telephone service savings were noted if certain equipment was purchased from the partner company.

Who was being conned? Not the customer. He saw through the "report" instantly because it was no more than a thinly veiled (and poorly prepared) gimmick to sell equipment. Did the phone company and its "partner" believe such a transparent, sophomoric approach could possibly succeed? If they did, they were only fooling themselves.

Stop getting in your own way.

If your objective is to make the sale, you render yourself ineffective as a salesperson. This is why more and more salespeople fail today. They're being told by their managers that the job is making sales. The president of a bank describes his company as a "sales organization." He knows exactly which products are profitable and easy to administer. There is only one problem—a dismal track record. He gets in his own way. Prospective customers recognize his objective. They sense that all he wants to do is make the sale. And no one buys.

Stop deciding who will become a customer.

Salespeople are taught to look for "buying signals." If they see them, there is a sale on the way. If not, it is time to move on. Such an approach is, of course, nonsense. The task is far more difficult today. Instead of getting the order, the objective must be to create the customer—someone who wants to do business with you.

Stop thinking you know what is best for the customer or what the customer wants.

The insurance agent says: "We would like to quote your insurance. I think we can save you money." Because the unsuspecting business managers always want to save money, they say, "Sure."

What happens next is most revealing. Chances are the salesperson will say, "All I need is your policies. How about if I pick them up tomorrow?" With this information, the agent will send off the current insurance program—including the premium costs—to a couple of insurance companies to see who comes back with the lowest price.

While customers like low prices, they also want their businesses protected. Unfortunately, the agent is just duplicating the previous agent's work that was probably the exact duplication of someone else's efforts. No one is looking carefully at the business to discover its exposures.

Stop being in such a hurry.

Sales professionals know that selling today is about patience and persistence—no matter what anyone else, including sales managers, might say or expect. This is what takes talent and skill. Hurrying or trying to rush prospects to buy simply does not work. In fact, it is a turnoff to customers because they recognize they are simply being used. No one likes that.

Today's expert salespeople are as adroit at managing many prospects as they are at managing accounts. They know that top prospects do not make quick decisions; they do not jump from one vendor to the other. These are the customers who will test a company and its sales reps before making a commitment. They write off anyone who comes on strong and then fades away because a deal is not signed quickly.

Stop forgetting who the center of attention is.

A customer went to the bank to cash in a U.S. savings bond. "We cannot do that ... the computer is down," were the first words out of the CSR's mouth.

A better focus might have been: "I will be glad to take care of that for you. At the moment, we are having computer problems. Can I call you to let you know when we are back online?"

The focus of attention may be the salesperson's highest hurdle. If you want a clue as to how salespeople view themselves, listen to their voice mail messages. "... I will get back to you as soon as I can." Or, "I am away from my desk right now; I will return your call as soon as I can."

Listen carefully. It is all about them ... not the person who is calling. Minor issue? Perhaps, and then again, perhaps not. Unconsciously, words often reflect our focus of attention.

> *John R. Graham is president of Graham Communications, a marketing services and sales consulting firm. He is the author of* Break the Rules Selling: Success Strategies That Beat the Competition, *and three other books on marketing and sales. Contact him at 617-328-0069 or through the company's website,* www.grahamcomm.com.

Know the right way to sell insurance.

Here are some attention-getting promotions, courtesy of the MDRT.

- Organize a group of successful local businesspeople to discuss and exchange ideas.

- Give a donation to a charity in your client's name.

- Send a small gift, such as a photo album, a baby spoon or flowers to clients who have recently had a baby or adopted a child. If the client is a new grandparent, do the same.

- Send a birthday cake to your clients.

- Make your business card stand out. One way is to model it after a baseball card with your photo on the front and your qualifications on the back.

(Reported by Chuck Jones, former senior editor of Advisor Today*)*

Beware of the myths that can threaten success in selling.

Selling is a tough job. If you sell, you are never finished. There is always the next customer, a problem to solve, a crisis need or a meeting to attend.

There is little opportunity for a salesperson to check out. The "antenna" must be up at all times, ready to detect the slightest indication of the unexpected. The strategizing never ends.

If sales is essentially a task of carefully identifying customer needs and meeting them, then much of the folklore and images surrounding selling are nothing more than useless baggage or myths that are passed from one generation of salespeople to the next as if they were sacred—and infallible truth.

In the current business and consumer environments, these myths inhibit salespeople from closing more sales. A place to begin rethinking selling is with the following myths:

A good salesperson knows how to push the customer's hot buttons. Anyone adept at selling focuses his attention on the customer and listens carefully for buying cues. Unfortunately, that is all many salespeople do. They do not attempt to probe and develop a larger perspective or a deeper understanding of the situation. Rather than working to meet the customer's needs, they stop with his wants. More often than not, these turn out to be "one-time" sales. It does not take much for the customer to figure out what was purchased and whether it failed either to satisfy his expectations or meet his objectives.

I know my customers like I know the back of my hand. Yesterday's salespeople often viewed themselves as "gatekeepers," as intermediaries between the company and the customers. While knowing customers is essential in selling, it is extremely dangerous to assume that knowing implies having a hold on the customer. You may know your customers, but you may not know what they are doing and thinking. While salespeople like to think they have the customer "under control," it is far more accurate to view today's customer as a "free agent" who is constantly making new discoveries and getting information easily, and one who does not feel beholden to a salesperson.

When it comes right down to it, it is always price. While there is always some price sensitivity, what customers really want is value for their dollar. However, this does not mean their only interest is price. If that were true, no one would be writing with a Mont Blanc pen. Agway Bagged Feeds is successful in selling dealers on its equine feeds against lower-priced competitive feeds because the company educates them about the differences in the products. Customers want value for their dollar. They expect to pay for the results they need. If they cannot differentiate one product or service from the other, it only makes sense for them to choose the one with the lowest price.

Selling is a game. The goal is to outsmart the buyer. Here is the most pervasive—and perhaps—the most destructive myth of all. It describes sales as a game. "Winning" is a matter of the salesperson outsmarting or outmaneuvering the customer—getting the best of the customer. Selling is more serious than a game. Sales is a process of aligning the resources made available by the salesperson with the needs of the customer. This takes skill, knowledge and competence.

Demythologizing sales may be the beginning of selling in the New Economy. Getting rid of dysfunctional myths sets a salesperson free to meet customer needs.

John R. Graham is president of Graham Communications, a marketing services and sales consulting firm. He is the author of Break the Rules Selling: Success Strategies That Beat the Competition, *and three other books on marketing and sales. Contact him at 617-328-0069 or through the company's website,* www.grahamcomm.com.

BUSINESS INSURANCE & RETIREMENT PLANNING

Make money the easy way. Learn Tom Wolff's buy/sell valuation system.

Do you want to write substantial amounts of business, which require very little work? I thought so, so I am sharing my buy/sell valuation system.

To illustrate, let me recreate a typical meeting among clients (who are about to enter into an agreement), their attorney and myself. The lawyer asks how much the company is worth. The clients respond they are not sure. The attorney appropriately responds: "Suppose you wanted to sell the company. A buyer who is willing to pay a fair price appears. How much would you ask?" The owners respond with a $1.5 million number. The attorney advises them to use that price as the initial valuation. Everyone agrees and $750,000 of life insurance on each owner is recommended to fund the agreement.

Next, we discuss future valuations and valuations at time of death. The attorney provides a number of options. These include:

- Book value

- Book value plus goodwill

- A multiple of revenues or profits

- Appointment of appraisers

All the foregoing negate one of the biggest advantages of a buy/sell: the ability of the owners, while alive, to determine a fair price. When an owner dies and the valuation is made under any of the foregoing scenarios, there is bound to be dissatisfaction.

At this point, I suggest a valuation schedule be attached to the agreement. Each year, the owners will decide on the appropriate value and endorse it on the schedule. I point out that heirs can hardly argue with the value the deceased agreed to. The attorney interrupts and asks, "But suppose they forget to revalue?"

I respond, "There should be a fail-safe provision in the agreement in the event that does happen. It should not come into play, however, because I'll accept the responsibility of reminding all parties annually that new values have to be endorsed on the schedule." During my 47-year career, I have been involved in hundreds of buy/sell situations. In most cases, I have prevailed on attorneys to do the agreement my way.

To make sure that I keep my promise, we establish a computer-based program. The two ingredients of the system are illustrated below.

The following letter goes out about 15 days prior to the anniversary date. We follow up with a telephone call reminding clients of the need to agree on a new value. Either on this call or on a subsequent call, the new value is given to us. We immediately arrange for the medical requirements and obtain the applications.

We've had dozens of death claims in which our advice has been followed. Yes, it is unfortunate that someone died, but the survivors have been grateful for the guidance we provided.

Dear Fellows:

Your buy/sell agreement provides that, on the 1st of April each year, you shall agree on the value of your stock. Once agreed upon, said value will be endorsed on Schedule C of your agreement. The most recent value is $15,000 per share or a total value of $1.5 million.

I will be in touch with you shortly to determine whether or not you consider this valuation to be adequate at this time.

cc: Your Advisors

Sample Situation

Attorney:	*George Small*
Accountant:	*Edward Anderson*
Entity:	*Corporation*
Type of Agreement:	*Stock Redemption*
Parties to Agreement:	*Lee Dunn and James Turner*
Date of Agreement:	*April 9*
Amendments:	*None*
Methods of payment of any excess over insurance proceeds:	*Installments–5 Years–Interest @ 10%*

Ownership:

Name	Number of shares	Percentage of whole
Lee Dunn	*50*	*50%*
James Turner	*50*	*50%*

Policies Issued:

Name	Company and no.	Amount and kind
Lee Dunn	*1496155*	*750,000 whole life*
James Turner	*1496156*	*750,000 whole life*

Method of Valuation:
Annually on April 1st. If none made in 24 months, CPA will determine book value and it shall prevail.

Thomas John Wolff, CLU, ChFC, served as president of NALU (NAIFA) from 1979-1980. A member of MDRT since 1958, he is a recipient of the John Newton Russell Award. His address: P.O. Box H, Vernon, CT 06066.

Don't just sell keyperson insurance; make the second sale with keyperson disability insurance.

Intellectually rich companies tend to be highly dependent on the human capital of one or two key leaders who drive shareholder value. Virtually all corporations respond to this risk by securing keyperson life insurance. But the greater risk is the exposure to a disabling injury or illness that prevents these leaders from executing their plans and realizing their vision.

Statistically, the risk of an individual suffering from a disability during his working years is significantly higher than the risk of death. A 45-year-old executive is three times more likely to suffer from a disability lasting more than 90 days than to die before age 65. In either event, the corporation faces significant loss. Why is it that less than 35 percent of all companies that secure keyperson life insurance coverage purchase the corresponding keyperson disability coverage?

In today's competitive business environment, protecting the value of a star executive is more critical than ever. Using markets once reserved for elite athletes and entertainers, carriers like Lloyd's of London and other domestic niche market players have developed keyperson disability products designed to protect a company's most critical assets.

These specialty carriers can deliver disability benefits exceeding $100,000 per month and lump-sum benefits of up to $100 million.

The following case study illustrates the importance of buying keyperson disability insurance: A global public relations firm purchased a highly successful "boutique" company. The acquisition was made by paying the two owners of the company in two parts. Part A was a cash payment upon close of the acquisition valued at approximately $10 million each. Part B was a cash payment made to each shareholder over time based on certain performance targets. The acquisition agreement called for $10 million of keyperson insurance on each owner. The intent of this provision was to secure keyperson life insurance. However, when the broker went back to the CFO and explained that the risk of disability was the greater exposure to the corporation, a second sale was made.

Ted Tafaro is a vice president of BISYS Insurance. Contact him at 800-443-2922 or ted.tafaro@BISYS.com.

Sell a low-hassle executive bonus plan to business owners.

An attractive fringe benefit for attracting and retaining key employees is permanent life insurance, which provides current protection through the policy's death benefit, along with a future source of retirement income using the policy's cash value.

This can be done with an executive bonus plan, in which the employee, or a trust set up by the employee, owns a life insurance policy for which the employer pays the premium. The employer can pay the premium directly to the insurance company or indirectly as a bonus to the employee. In either case, Section 162 of the Internal Revenue Code permits the employer to deduct the amount of the premium, as long as the employee's total compensation meets the IRS guideline of "reasonable" and the employer has no ownership interest in the insurance policy.

Because the amount of the premium is considered to be a bonus, it is included in the employee's gross income. However, some employers will pay an extra bonus to cover applicable taxes.

An added feature is that the executive bonus plan is not subject to non-discrimination rules; therefore, the employer can designate who will receive the benefit and how much they will receive. The only restriction is the IRS definition of reasonable compensation. In fact, no IRS approval is needed, nor is any burdensome reporting required.

One concern to employers is that the employee owns the policy and can leave with it at any time. To extend some measure of control over the policy, the employer can:

- Add a restrictive endorsement limiting the employee's use of the cash value until a specified time or number of years.

- Create an employment contract requiring an employee to repay the amount of the bonus in part or in full as stipulated by a vesting schedule.

- When extending control, make sure you understand the effect a specific strategy may have on the employer's ability to take a current tax deduction.

(Due to its legal nature, placing restrictions on an executive bonus plan should be done in consultation with a qualified attorney.)

Kirk Okumura is an LUTC author and editor. Contact him at kirko@amercoll.edu.

Use an executive bonus plan to lower business taxes for C corporation owners.

Because owners of C corporations are considered employees, they can use an executive bonus plan to purchase their personal insurance. (With the bonus plan, the employee, which in this case is also the owner—or a trust he sets up—owns a life insurance policy for which the "employer" pays the premium.) This makes sense when the corporation's tax bracket is higher than the owner's personal tax bracket. This commonly happens when the owner is in the 30-percent tax bracket or lower, and his or her corporation is in the 34-percent tax bracket. Because of an anomaly in the tax code, taxable income between $100,000 and $335,000 for corporations is taxed at 39 percent. Thus, owners in the 30-percent personal income-tax bracket may be able to save between 4 percent and 9 percent in corporate income taxes by using an executive bonus plan to purchase their personal insurance.

Kirk Okumura is an LUTC author and editor. Contact him at kirko@amercoll.edu.

Break into the SBA-guaranteed loan market.

When a business owner applies for a Small Business Administration-guaranteed loan, he normally goes to a bank or an SBA-approved nonbank lender. Both of these entities require life insurance on the loan signers.

This is an underserved market and a wonderful opportunity to increase the face amount of the insurance policies sold. A business owner who secures an SBA-guaranteed loan is usually in good financial shape and poised for growth. This means other potential sales in the future. In addition, this business owner probably plans to continue growing her business and will need future, larger loans (and larger insurance policies) to do so.

To save a client the hassles of applying for subsequent, small policies, I suggested that she apply for the maximum coverage available to her without increasing the underwriting requirements. After all, she could always decline the extra coverage at the time of issue. As I put it: "Ms. Client, are you planning to grow your business in the future? Do you want to take the time to do the paperwork for more insurance to make the lender happy? If not, I know a way to 'pre-insure' for your future growth." It has worked for me—I turned a $175,000 first-to-die sale on five insureds into a $250,000 one.

Janet Arrowood is the managing director of The Write Source, Inc. Contact her at jcarrow427@earthlink.net.

Woo the small-business owner with a checklist of critical questions.

To sell more and larger cases to small-business owners, use these questions as marketing and sales opportunities:

Question: Have you ever had your business valued?
Related question: Was this a formal valuation by an experienced professional?
Marketing/sales opportunity: Most business owners have no idea what their business is really worth, and it is never a good idea to let the IRS establish the value, but that is exactly what many business owners do. Offer to refer the owner to a CPA or appraisal specialist.

Question: Do you have a buy/sell agreement?
Related questions: How is it funded? Who prepared it? When was it last reviewed?
Marketing/sales opportunity: Few clients want to be in business with their co-owners' heirs. If a buy/sell agreement exists and is unfunded, the business may have to be sold at fire-sale prices just to pay the estate

of the deceased owner. Ask for a copy of the buy/sell agreement and funding mechanism. Ask for permission to call the advisors who created it. Make sure the buy/sell agreement includes disability buy-out and disability-income provisions and get those provisions funded.

Question: Do you have a way to replace keypersons or owners if they die?

Related questions: What would happen if your chief "X" died? How would you replace him/her?

Marketing/sales opportunity: Ask for a copy of the replacement and funding plan. There probably isn't one.

Question: Do you have insurance to protect your income, pay your obligations for business expenses or buy out a disabled owner?

Related questions: What do you consider your most valuable asset? How would you get by without your income or business?

Marketing/sales opportunity: Offer to prepare illustrations of the various disability options: income, buy-out and overhead expense. Explain what each type does and does not cover.

Question: Do you have a funded, qualified retirement plan?

Related question: Are you getting the most from your own and your company's contributions?

Marketing/sales opportunity: Congress has enacted some generous new provisions that favor business owners while benefiting employees, including: Roth contributions inside many 401(k) and 403(b) plans, increasing limits for retirement plans, and comparability provisions in profit-sharing plans so participants who are more highly paid receive greater benefits. Provide a matrix showing the "comparability" profit-sharing plan and Roth options. Emphasize the present and future tax savings and income needs.

Go to every client or prospect meeting with a checklist so that you don't overlook key needs. Develop your own checklist, get it approved

by your broker-dealer and general agent where applicable, ask every question on the list and get your client or prospect to sign the list. Leave a copy with the client or prospect.

> *Janet Arrowood is the managing director of The Write Source, Inc. Contact her at* jcarrow427@earthlink.net.

Remind your clients of the consequences of not making proper arrangements for the future of their business.

"Do you want your partner's wife or her second husband to be your partner in this business?" I ask my business clients when I am trying to get them to realize the need for buy-out insurance.

Many of my clients are in the real-estate development business. Reminding them of the consequences of not making proper arrangements for the future of the business, I ask, "Why be forced to liquidate your property or make arrangements to pay off the government over a period of years at a very high interest rate? I will charge you only 2 cents to provide 100 cents of what is needed, and you will never have to pay the 100 cents back. You do not want to have to go to a bank or mortgage your property. Consider the advantages of my proposal."

> *Mitchell Ostrove, CLU, of White Plains, N.Y., can be reached at 914-428-4095 or* mitch@ostrovegroup.com.

Make a gross comparison.

In business-continuation planning, compare the gross sales required to generate enough net profit to fund the buy/sell agreement with the gross sales and net profit required using life insurance. In most cases, paying the premium is less than using your own profits or borrowing the money.

This is an excellent way to illustrate how the survivors can purchase the business at a discount. Just asking the business owner what the net profit to gross sales ratio is during the factfinding process will give you the needed information.

Cliff F. Wilson, CLU, ChFC, LUTCF, is a NAIFA trustee. He is with Southeast Arizona Agency in Chandler, Ariz. You may reach him at 480-969-2725.

Use direct mail to spark interest in business owners.

I mail letters to business owners. These letters show yearly renewable term rates for 35- to 65-year-old male nonsmokers for policies ranging from $250,000 to $3 million. I include a reply form and an envelope, and I ask for date of birth, tobacco use, and the best time that I can call them. I rarely call unless they respond.

These letters generate interest from all kinds of people and lead to sales not only for term but also for whole life, disability, keyperson and so on. Some are interested in discussing only the term insurance policy, but many allow me to do a full factfinder.

This is another way of building rapport, and some of my best clients responded to one of those letters.

Charles T. Weaver, CSH, LUTCF, is with 50+ Financial Solutions in Nashville, Tenn. You may reach him at 615-227-1011.

Tell your clients to cash in, not cash out.

Here is a retirement funding idea. When your client says he wants to cash out his insurance, suggest the advantages of keeping the insurance in force by electing paid-up insurance at age 65. Then change the dividend option to an annuity to supplement his retirement income. The advantages are tax-free growth during the accumulation period, tax-free death benefit throughout, waiver of premium benefits to 65, and cash value to be borrowed against without penalty after the 15th year.

Malcolm English, LUTCF, of the MONY Life Insurance Company in Hattiesburg, Miss., can be reached at 601-268-3983.

Let your clients know that they can have tax-free income from their life insurance contracts.

I sell clients on the idea that they can have tax-free income from their life insurance contract. I tell them that when they are ready to retire, they are going to have to pay taxes on their pension. And I ask, "Wouldn't it be nice to have something you don't have to pay taxes on?"

Companies have universal life policies that allow you to borrow the cash value and almost have a zero loan on a 1 percent difference between what you are earning and what you are getting.

If the client has $200,000, he might get $15,000 a year for the rest of his life from age 65 to 95. And he pays no taxes on that amount.

I tell him that he is looking at a minimum insurance expense but a maximum benefit at the end.

William D. Barnes of William D. Barnes & Associates in Tampa, Fla., can be reached at 813-968-6181 or bbarnesandco@aol.com.

Learn the recipe for the retirement cake ... so your clients can have their cake and eat it, too.

How large a nest egg will it take to retire comfortably? Will your investment capital run out before you do? What is the right investment mix for a long retirement—maybe 20 or 30 years or more? An advisor who can answer these questions will be an invaluable resource to clients starved for answers.

Maybe this recipe for a retirement cake will help answer some of the questions. First, grab a mixing bowl from the kitchen cupboard. Then, pull three mutual funds off the pantry shelf. Stir in one growth and income fund, one long-term growth fund and one international fund. Or, season to taste as your tolerance for risk will allow. Cooking with the best ingredients helps ensure the best result, so select funds that have lower expenses and risk. Mix the ingredients thoroughly, reinvesting all dividends and capital gains. Pour the contents into a baking pan and let them bake in the oven for 20 years.

All good chefs, of course, need to periodically taste their creations. So every year, reach in the oven with a big cooking spoon and scoop out 9 percent of the cake. Because your appetite grows, increase the size of your scoop by 3 percent each year.

Twenty years later, the timer rings, announcing that your cake is done. So you open the oven door and pull out the remaining cake. But something strange has happened! You pull out more cake than the original ingredients you put in 20 years ago—more cake than you tasted each year along the way. You have baked a retirement cake that will feed its owner for 20 years, and there will still be plenty left over for seconds or thirds.

James P. Ruth, CFP, is a registered representative and president of Potomac Financial Group in Gaithersburg, Md. Contact him at 301-948-3900 or at jruth@pfgroup.org.

DISABILITY INCOME INSURANCE

Follow these five steps to success in selling disability income insurance.

1. Target professionals and small-business owners.

2. Tell real-life stories and use a lot of empathy.

3. Disability income insurance is seen as expensive so learn how to overcome a prospect's objections.

4. Know the types of coverage your prospects need.

5. Offer supplemental plans.

(Reported in Advisor Today*)*

Point out the gap in your client's disability policy.

Sometimes people who have a need for more than one kind of insurance do not want to talk about more than one product at a time. In that case, when I deliver the life insurance policy to them, I will point out the gap in their disability coverage and offer to help them close it.

If they balk at my suggestion, I say to them:

"Well, let me put it this way. Let's say I am a doctor and you have come to me complaining of a pain in your side. I examine you, determine you have appendicitis and take out your appendix. But if I also notice you have a problem with gallstones, and I do nothing about it, you are still going to come back to me complaining of pain. It was unprofessional of me not to tell you about the other problem. This is a similar situation. You have another problem in your financial portfolio that will not go away unless we address it. It would be unprofessional of me not to bring it to your attention."

Harry Lee of MONY, in Tuscaloosa, Ala., can be contacted at 205-752-0494 or at hlee@mony.com.

Suggest the option-to-purchase insurance policy to your clients.

One of the easiest disability income insurance sales I know is the option-to-purchase insurance. This option guarantees the availability of additional disability income insurance into the future without evidence of insurability (only evidence of income). This is an easy sale over the telephone, no fuss, no muss. It is a responsible action by the agent to make sure a client's coverage is updated in keeping with increasing income. I call my clients annually to make sure they keep up with their coverage. It is an excellent source of income without a lot of work. I have made over $2,500 in commission just as a result of a single phone call.

Prudence A. Harker, CFP, ChFC, CLU, RHU, of LifeCircle in South Beloit, Ill., can be reached at 608-365-2115.

Ask a prospect if his group long-term disability plan is discriminatory.

I use disability income insurance to get into business doors because, quite frankly, there are very few people doing it. I get the business-person's interest by asking him the following question: "Is your group long-term disability plan discriminatory?" Typically, they will answer, "No, of course not. That would be illegal."

Then I would say: "I do not mean if it discriminates against the rank-and-file employees. I am asking if it discriminates against the owners of the company. I bet it does."

It is very easy to show business prospects that under a typical group, long-term disability plan in which you have a formula of 60 percent of income up to a maximum of $3,000 a month, that plan will replace 60 percent of the income of almost everyone in the company except the owners and top executives. With them, it may replace only 30 percent to 40 percent of their income. That is discrimination and the only way to overcome it is with individual disability income insurance policies.

John Marshall, CLU, ChFC, is a principal with Alcos Inc. in Sterling Heights, Mich. You may reach him at 586-977-6300.

Sell executives a disability income insurance plan that pays about three-quarters of their income and an accelerated life plan.

For your executive prospects who want a 100 percent disability plan, sell them a regular disability plan that pays about three-quarters of their income should they become disabled. Also sell them an accelerated life plan that provides at least a 25 percent payout in the event of a heart attack, cancer, diabetes or other catastrophic illness.

Donald Wingate, LUTCF, is with Monumental Life Insurance Co. in Chester, S.C. He can be reached at 803-347-5455.

Teach small businesses the true reality of disability risk.

What can advisors do to increase their chances of making a disability income insurance sale to small businesses? Simply put: Clear the air. Teaching small-business owners the true reality of disability risk can pave the way to relationship building and selling opportunities.

To gain further ground with small-business owners, advisors must acknowledge and work with the shadow that medical, dental and retirement benefits cast over DI insurance in the workplace. "The medical environment in particular is very difficult," says UNUM Managing Consultant David Sherman. "Employers are looking at 20 to 40 percent cost increases. With increases like that, DI doesn't get time or attention in staff benefits meetings," or in sales calls with advisors.

Savvy advisors will make this difficult climate work to their advantage. "Employers are passing off health-insurance cost increases and copays to employees," says Sherman. "Offering a DI plan can help offset some of the bad feelings among employees who are seeing these benefits either go out the window or increase in cost significantly." Many competent agents and brokers that Sherman works with are successfully using this approach with their small-business clients.

In addition, with the DI insurance market becoming increasingly competitive, carriers are adding incentives to their DI insurance proposals. These incentives can make a small-business owner look benevolent, even in the wake of increased employee contributions to other insurance coverage. "Many small employers can get an EAP (employee assistance program) or a travel-assistance program as part of their DI plan as an incentive, free of charge. So they can offer all three at a relatively low cost. A lot of small employers don't know about this."

DI insurance has many benefits advisors can present to help soften the resistance of small businesses. The bottom line is they must create the need for DI insurance by helping employers understand the very real risk of disability.

(Reported by Lucretia DiSanto Jones, financial services editor of Advisor Today)

The golden spouse

Ask families with two wage earners the following question: "Are you banking all the money your spouse is making? If not, you must be using it for your living expenses.

"If your spouse becomes disabled, what will that do to your living standard? Will you still be able to pay your bills? Let me show you how easy it is to make sure your loss will be covered when that happens."

Eleanor K. Peterson, CLU, ChFC, is with Eastern Planned Incomes in New York. You may reach her at 315-682-4828.

Help the prospect see the need.

The sales approach for disability income insurance is similar to that used for life insurance—help the prospect see the need, then show

how your product meets the need. Sell the benefits, not the policy features. Talk about what the benefits buy, not how much they cost.

Start by making a discussion of DI protection part of every interview you have. Make it a critical part of developing the advisor-client relationship.

When you deliver a life policy with waiver of premium, try this approach. When you review the policy with the client, save the explanation of the waiver of premium until last. When you've explained the waiver and how it works, ask your client, "Do you have that feature on your mortgage?" Of course, the answer is no. You can reply, "The waiver of premium feature protects the investment you've made in your life insurance. How would you like that same feature for your mortgage?"

When you close a homeowner's or auto policy sale, tell the client: "Now that we've taken care of your home, I'd like to talk to you about your most valuable asset."

Tapping businesses

If you are already active in the business market, have you discussed disability protection with your business clients? If a group policy is already in place, you should review its limits and develop carve-out proposals for the owners and executives. If group coverage is not in place, propose a group plan.

One advantage of working through businesses is that each interview creates a number of sales opportunities. Business owners who are not interested in providing group coverage may see the importance of individual coverage for themselves. They may also see the advantage of offering their employees access through a voluntary program, making the entire workforce your prospects. You benefit by being able to see a number of prospects in a favorable environment. And with a well-planned presentation, you can explain the basic elements of the coverage in a group meeting, using private interviews to focus on individual needs.

Building on the preconceived idea that DI protection is a work-related benefit, you can develop both business and individual clients. Business clients, recognizing the value of DI insurance as an employee benefit, can be approached for group sales or they can be used as an open door for voluntary group list billing or payroll deduction programs. This is an approach used extensively by Tim Moran, LUTCF, of the UCL Financial Group in Memphis. Moran's disability sales make up 25 percent to 30 percent of his total volume.

"People get phone calls at home all the time," he says, "but with a payroll deduction program, I get to see them one-on-one all in a day or two. And the employer gets the credit for sponsoring the program."

Moran also sees the tendency toward voluntary instead of employer-paid programs. And he sees the continued opportunity for traditional carve-out programs, filling the gap that often exists between group coverage and the income needs of employees with high incomes.

If you work primarily in the personal market, a DI insurance approach may open the door to the business market. Do reviews with existing clients covered by employer-sponsored groups to make sure their coverage is adequate. If it isn't, and a gap exists between a group policy's cap and the amount the client needs, you can fill the need with a personal policy.

If no group coverage exists, both the client and the employer are prospects. You can use the client's need as an opportunity to approach the employer about creating the opportunity to install either a voluntary or group plan.

You have to ask

Whether the approach is in the workplace or at home, with new prospects or existing clients, the basics are the same. The sale doesn't just happen. An advisor has to ask.

Meridee Maynard, CPA, PFS, CFP, CLU, ChFC, Northwestern Mutual's vice president of DI insurance, suggests this approach: Ask your prospect to write down six things—not people—that are very important to them. Usually the list will include health and income, along with personal assets. Ask him to pick two of the six. Most people will pick health and income. Ask if he has insured his health. Almost everyone understands how important it is to have health insurance. Then ask if he has insured his income.

Richard Weikart, CLU, ChFC, is a principal in Weikart & Williams, LLC, a training design and development firm in the Washington, D.C., area. You can reach him at rweikart@comcast.net.

ESTATE PLANNING

Use one of my favorite "Feldmanisms."

Insurance great Ben Feldman was trying to sell insurance to fund a buy/sell agreement. The firm's accountant was in attendance. He observed that the client did not need to fund the buy/sell since they would be saving the deceased's salary if one partner died. The debt to the deceased's family could be paid with these savings.

Ben turned to one partner and said, "Jim, they don't think much of you. They don't believe you earn your pay!" Then turning to the other owner, he asked, "Has Jim ever been away?"

"Yes, he has," came the answer.

"Did you miss him?"

"I sure did."

"Suppose he walked out and never came back? Would you miss him?"

"It would be tough."

"He is a key man, isn't he? He has stubbed his toes over the years and has earned because of it, and that's why he is so good," Ben pointed out. "You'd have to replace him. The new man wouldn't be as good for two reasons. One, he wouldn't own the business, and two, he'd have to stub his toes for awhile. That's why he'd earn less because he'd be

worth less. And if you only lost in profits what you saved between Jim's pay and his replacement's pay, you'd be pretty happy, wouldn't you?"

"I guess so," the partner replied.

"So you wouldn't save anything but you'd still have to pay off the debt, right?"

"I guess so."

"You know, it will get worse before it gets better. What would you say your annual rate of growth has been?"

"About 8 percent."

"If Jim lives nine years and then dies, you'll need twice as much money to buy him out."

Ned B. Ricks, CLU, is a managing member of Guidon Consulting, LLC, in Gurnee, Ill. Contact him at 847-856-8826 or at NedR0003@aol.com.

Buy immortality in the hearts of your grandchildren.

Now that my contemporaries are now grandparents or great grandparents, I approach them with a gift idea guaranteeing they will be remembered long after they are gone.

I say something like this: "I want to talk to you about buying immortality in the hearts of your grandchildren. You give your grandchildren gifts from time to time. But most of these are transient. Here is a gift that will last far beyond your years. Let's talk about a gift of life insurance—a policy with a premium substantially less than can be obtained by them later, one where the dividend may one day take over paying that premium. Someday, your grandchildren will need life insurance for their families. Far in the future, after you and I are long gone, your grandchildren will receive notices from the insurance company every year telling them that the premium is already paid through the dividends of the policy itself. What's more, even though the protection is provided without their paying a penny out-of-pocket, the values continue to increase each year."

Bernard H. (Buddy) Zais, CLU, ChFC, is with Massachusetts Mutual in Burlington, Vermont. (802-658-2930)

Get prospects to commit to their priorities during the first minutes of the interview.

When working with an estate-planning prospect, I used to have problems at the close when we started to talk about the cost of insurance premiums. People want to help their children as long as it doesn't cost them anything.

To solve this problem up front, I make them commit to their priorities during our first minutes together by writing in big letters on a sheet of paper: children, charity and Uncle Sam.

I hand them the paper and pen and ask them to write one, two and three next to these words in the order in which they want their money to go. I won't proceed until they've done it. This exercise solves the question of whether it's OK to have their children inherit $2 million while Uncle Sam gets $1 million.

Donald R. Burkall, CLU, ChFC, is with Northwestern Mutual Financial Network in Chapel Hill, N.C. Contact him at 919-401-0323 or at don.burkall@nmfn.com.

Sell the annual gift-tax exclusion.

I have found the annual gift-tax exclusion to be a rich source of premium payments for life insurance, whether it is on an individual life policy or a survivorship life policy.

The track runs like this: "Mr. Prospect, the use of the annual gift-tax exclusion is the most overlooked area in estate planning today."

When the prospect asks what I mean, I say, "Most people aren't taking advantage of their right to give $11,000 a year to their children. We can use that $11,000 to pay the estate taxes on your wealth in discounted dollars. Doesn't that make sense?"

Charles D. Marks, CLU, ChFC, is a consultant in New Orleans. Contact him at 504-586-8741 or cdmdrt@msn. com.

Immortalize tithes.

This is an idea I use to help people who go to church and want to immortalize their tithes. I recommend a joint survivor life policy on the husband and wife and suggest they appoint a trustee. Twelve months after the last owner of the contract dies, the interest on that contract will be paid to the church every year indefinitely. If it is a $100,000 policy earning 10 percent interest, the church will receive $10,000 every year as a gift from those clients.

M. Jack Peckinpaugh, CLU, ChFC, LUTCF, is a partner in Peckinpaugh Beasley in Muncie, Ind. Contact him at 765-287-8310 or peckbeas@comcast.net.

LIFE INSURANCE

Sell life insurance as an estate equalizer.

Most parents want to treat their children equally when dividing up their estate. But this may prove impractical in those situations where the estate includes assets that are earmarked for only some of the children. A typical example is a family business in which only the children active in the business are to receive the business. If the business' value exceeds the active children's share of the estate, it is impossible to treat the children equally.

A simple solution is to use a life insurance policy as an estate equalizer. The children who are not active would be the beneficiaries of the policy. This not only helps ensure business continuation, but also helps to preserve family harmony.

Julius H. Giarmarco is with Cox, Hodgman & Giarmarco, P.C. Contact him at 101 W. Big Beaver Road, 10th Floor, Troy, MI 48084, at 248-457-7200 or jhg@disinherit-irs. com.

Sell single-premium immediate annuity contracts to risk-averse clients and prospects.

Many people who are averse to the stock market's daily fluctuations prefer to park their investments in municipal bonds or certificates of deposit (CDs). However, they gain a very low yield in exchange for their security. In many cases, a better alternative to municipal bonds and CDs is a single-premium immediate annuity contract.

Not only is the annuity a safe investment, it invariably will produce a significantly higher yield than municipal bonds or CDs. The problem with an annuity is that the payments cease when the annuitant dies. Accordingly, unlike the case with muni-bonds or CDs, the annuity owner's children will not inherit the annuity. The solution is to purchase a life insurance policy to "replace" the wealth lost when the annuitant dies. The cash to pay the premiums is generated from the increased cash flow that results from "converting" the muni-bonds and CDs into an annuity.

Julius H. Giarmarco is with Cox, Hodgman & Giarmarco, P.C. Contact him at 101 W. Big Beaver Road, 10th Floor, Troy, MI 48084, at 248-457-7200 or jhg@disinherit-irs. com.

Sell life insurance to businesses assuming the risk of potential environmental contamination.

Businesses assuming the risk of potential environmental contamination (i.e., waste hauling, landfills, chemicals, etc.) are subject to liability under federal and state pollution laws. What's more, such liability is not limited to the business itself, as the business owners also may be personally liable under such laws.

While these businesses may be risky, they also can be profitable. Therefore, many business owners falling into this category would still like to see the business passed on to younger family members. Of course, as the business passes to the next generation, so does the potential liability.

Life insurance is a perfect solution to this problem. The business owner can establish an irrevocable trust to run for the maximum period permitted by state law (i.e., at least 90 years in most states and in perpetuity in a handful of others). These often are referred to as dynasty trusts.

The trust would own a life insurance policy on the business owner's life. The trust would provide the business owner's children, grand-children and even great-grandchildren with income and principal as needed for health, education, maintenance and support. If properly structured, the assets in the trust cannot be reached by the beneficia-ries' creditors, including state and federal environmental agencies.

> *Julius H. Giarmarco is with Cox, Hodgman & Giarmarco, P.C. Contact him at 101 W. Big Beaver Road, 10th Floor, Troy, MI 48084, at 248-457-7200 or* jhg@disinherit-irs. com.

Sell life insurance as a way to help pay for long-term nursing care.

For a person to become eligible for Medicaid to pay for his nursing home care, he must have income and assets below frightfully low levels.

But what about those persons with substantial assets who are not eligible for Medicaid? What options are available to them to protect their assets from the high cost of long-term nursing care?

First, at least 36 months before applying for Medicaid, the recipient can "divest" himself by gifting away all of his assets to children and grandchildren. However, many people reject the idea of gifting away most of their assets to become eligible for Medicaid. Second, long-term care insurance can be purchased to pay for such care. LTCI premiums, however, increase dramatically for people over age 65.

A better answer may be to buy life insurance. If the insured goes into a nursing home and must use private funds to pay for such care, eventually the insurance proceeds will replace the assets spent on nursing home care. Life insurance ensures that the insured's heirs are not disinherited by the high cost of long-term nursing care. If the insured never goes into a nursing home, upon his death, his heirs will receive a larger inheritance.

Julius H. Giarmarco is with Cox, Hodgman & Giarmarco, P.C. Contact him at 101 W. Big Beaver Road, 10th Floor, Troy, MI 48084, at 248-457-7200 or jhg@disinherit-irs. com.

Sell life insurance to people in second marriages.

When children from a previous marriage are involved, estate planning becomes much more complicated. Let's take the example of a second marriage where the husband has children from a previous marriage. It is not uncommon for the husband to want his wife to be the primary beneficiary of his estate, but with some assurances that when his wife dies, whatever remains of his estate passes to his children. How can this result be accomplished?

The husband can establish a living trust that, upon his death, provides his wife with income and principal as needed to maintain her standard of living, with the remainder passing to his children at his wife's death. This approach, however, has two problems. First, the children have to wait until their stepmother's death to inherit their father's wealth. This is particularly troublesome where the stepmother is close in age to the children.

Second, as the remainder beneficiaries of the trust, the children have legal rights to challenge the distributions from the trust to their stepmother if those distributions exceed (in the children's opinion) the amount called for by the trust. Many second spouses prefer not to be put in such a compromising position.

A possible solution to these problems is life insurance on the husband's life. The policy beneficiaries can be either the wife or the children. If the wife is the beneficiary, the husband can simply leave his estate to his children at his death. Alternatively, if the children are the beneficiaries of the policy, the husband can leave his estate to his wife outright. In either case, the second wife and the children from the first marriage will have no financial involvement with one another after the husband's death.

Julius H. Giarmarco is with Cox, Hodgman & Giarmarco, P.C. Contact him at 101 W. Big Beaver Road, 10th Floor, Troy, MI 48084, at 248-457-7200 or jhg@disinherit-irs. com.

Sell a survivorship life policy to a client with a special-needs child.

It is estimated that one in every 10 families has a developmentally disabled child. Such children often are eligible for Supplemental Security Income. SSI is a federally funded program administered by the states that provides payment for shelter, food and incidental expenses. SSI eligibility generally is accompanied by the eligibility for Medicaid, which provides medical care.

Many parents are skeptical about the future of the SSI and Medicaid programs. As a result, they establish, at the death of the surviving parent, a "special-needs" trust for the benefit of the disabled child. A special-needs trust is designed to supplement SSI and Medicaid, without disqualifying the child from any government assistance.

Unfortunately, the special-needs trust strategy provides little consolation to those parents who do not have funds to provide for their disabled child. Nor does it help parents who eventually would have to disinherit the rest of their children to provide adequately for the disabled child.

An easy solution to both of these problems is for the parents of the disabled child to purchase a survivorship life insurance policy. This policy would be owned by the parents, and payable to a special needs trust for the benefit of the disabled child at the surviving parent's death. Upon the death of the disabled child, before the complete distribution of the trust, the assets remaining in the trust could pass to the children who are not disabled or their descendants.

Julius H. Giarmarco is with Cox, Hodgman & Giarmarco, P.C. Contact him at 101 W. Big Beaver Road, 10th Floor, Troy, MI 48084, at 248-457-7200 or jhg@disinherit-irs. com.

Insure your clients' equities losses with term life insurance.

Almost everyone who has had a loss in the stock market was counting on their principal plus the increase to feather their nest eggs. Now it may take up to 20 years to regain what people have lost at current interest assumptions.

The solution is to insure the loss with a 20-year level term policy. If the investor dies anytime in the next 20 years, he will have his current investments, plus a death benefit. One client's investments were in high-tech and telecommunication industry stocks. He is currently $989,000 below his original investment.

We wrote a 20-year level term policy to cover this loss. Now he has bought time to recover his losses.

William L. Moore, CLU, ChFC, is with Kinder Brothers International in Dallas. Contact him at 972-380-0747 or wl.moore@attglobal.net

Show prospects the true value of life insurance.

If a prospect is still not convinced of the need for life insurance, I show him an application form from a local fast-food restaurant and put it down next to an insurance application.

"Life is full of choices," I say. "If you do not fill out a life insurance application today, you may find yourself having to fill out another application form at age 65. Or your loved ones will. Live, die or become disabled, life insurance is the cornerstone of financial independence."

Leslie W. Lee, CLU, ChFC, of Farmer Financial Services in Middleton, Wis., can be reached at 608-831-4857 or leslee@itis.com.

Learn about the many uses of life insurance you can share with your prospects and clients.

As you try to convince your prospects to buy life insurance, keep in mind that life insurance can be used to:

- Fund a buy/sell agreement.

- Secure a line of credit.

- Protect a business from monetary loss.

- Provide an employee benefit.

- Pay for college.

- Give money to charity.

- Create an estate.

- Pay estate taxes.

- Equalize an inheritance.

- Provide income.

- Guarantee future insurability.

(Reported by Chuck Jones, former senior editor of Advisor Today*)*

LONG-TERM CARE INSURANCE

When selling long-term care insurance, try to close during your first call.

When selling LTCI to seniors, it's important to close during your first call. If you have to come back again, the client has often forgotten most of what you have said, as LTCI is complex. And procrastination exposes the prospect to risk, too. An older person's health can change fast, making him high risk or uninsurable.

When you follow a proven process, closing is the easiest part of the sale.

1. Warm your prospects up with small talk about their situation and family. Next, ask detailed questions about their health. Write their answers down. When prospects see their health conditions on paper, it helps them focus on why you are there.

2. Use trial or assumptive closes at several points, which are designed to bring up possible objections. Then, when you get to the end, the prospect will have few or no objections, and you can close your sale easily.

3. Create awareness of the need for LTCI. Ask your prospects: "What are your plans when your health changes?" This question will help you open up their thoughts and feelings about long-term care. You might ask them if they have had any experience with long-term care in their families. Most

people want to protect their retirement savings and want to be able to get care at home, not become a burden on their children. They need to understand that private insurance is the most effective vehicle to accomplish their goals.

4. Show your prospects how they can pay for insurance, based on their assets and income. This removes the objection, "I can't afford it."

5. Go through the product brochure. Always stay in an assumptive-close mode when you do this. You never want to ask, "Would you like to buy this policy?" You're always assuming that they will buy, and it's simply a matter of selecting the best policy and most appropriate coverage. One trial close is, "Can you see how this feature would work when your health changes?" And use a yellow high-lighter when you go through the brochure. (If your compliance department says you cannot, give the highlighter to the prospect.) Once you've finished talking about the product, the client will review the brochure while you are preparing a rate comparison. His eyes will naturally go to the highlighted areas, and he'll understand the key points.

6. Ask him: "Do you have any questions?" at key points during the sales call. This will expose any objections and allow you to resolve them. Every time you answer a question, you're getting the prospect's permission to go forward, and his resistance will continue to decrease. An unanswered objection will stick in the prospect's mind, and he won't listen to anything else you're saying. When it comes time to close, you'll have an uphill battle.

By probing and asking questions, you engage the client in the sale. Don't do all the talking; make sure he is a participant in the sale.

Wilma Anderson is an LTCI sales trainer and producer in Littleton, Colo. Contact her at 720-344-0312 or at wilma@TheLTCcoach.com.

Sell long-term care insurance to the appropriate people.

Do you think it is difficult to sell LTCI? Maybe you're approaching the wrong person.

Think about the person who will provide the care if Medicaid doesn't, and there isn't enough money for the person to go into a suitable care facility or to pay for home care. In many states, adult children are required to help their parents financially if they have the means to do so. This often means it is the adult female children who will end up providing an exhausting level of care. As a result, these are the people you might want to approach.

When you approach them, ask a few simple questions:

- Do you think Medicare pays for your aging parents' long-term care needs? (Answer: Only if it's medically necessary care, and then only after a three-night hospital stay—not just three days.)

- Do your parents want to be separated and assigned a roommate in order to have Medicaid pay for nursing home care—assuming they even qualify financially?

- Are you financially or physically able to care for your aging parents?

These are three issues many prospects have not thought about and making them aware can go a long way toward making the sale.

Janet Arrowood is the managing director of The Write Source, Inc. Contact her at jcarrow427@earthlink.net.

Here are ways to help prospects pay for long-term care insurance.

While everyone would like to have LTCI, many people say, "I can't afford it." That's understandable, because LTCI is expensive. A typical benefit package—$200 per day for up to three years after a 100-day elimination period, with inflation protection—on average costs about $2,200 per year at age 60 and $4,450 at age 70. What many people don't realize is, it can be more expensive not to have it.

Despite the cost, most people who think they can't afford the coverage actually can afford it. As the advisor, you must find a plan that fits the client's budget and then find the money to pay for it.

To do this, you need to know how much money and income the prospect has to work with. One way to find out is to ask him: "If a nursing home costs $4,000 per month, how long would your savings last before you'd need to sell your home to pay for nursing home care?"

If the answer is about three-and-a-half years, that translates to about $170,000. Then ask him what interest rate he is earning. Let's say it's 5 percent, which translates into $8,500 each year.

Now you must find a policy with a premium that's equal to a portion of your client's interest earnings because most retirees need at least some of their interest for living expenses. Now you can compare premiums on different benefit packages.

While a lifetime benefit is best, statistics show that most people don't need long-term care for more than three years; so choosing a limited benefit period is a viable way to save money. Give the prospects quotes for two policies that offer an unlimited benefit and for policies that offer a two- or three-year benefit period.

Save money for 70-year-olds

Another way to save money for applicants in their 70s and older is to omit inflation protection. This is a reasonable choice because these clients most likely use their benefits within a few years.

However, with younger applicants, I always recommend buying inflation protection. It's too risky for the client (and the agent) to try to guess what long-term care might cost 20 or more years from now. Also unwise is to try to save money by using a lower-rated company.

Lower benefit amounts and longer elimination periods also save money. However, if the client chooses a benefit that's unlikely to cover the full cost of care, it's wise to set up a health fund he can use to partially self-insure the cost of care. With the money saved on lower premiums, the client can invest in a fixed or variable deferred annuity. I don't like immediate annuities because they lock the client into a fairly low interest rate. Deferred annuities are much more flexible, and in case of a medical emergency, the client can always withdraw money without penalty.

Once you and your client have at least tentatively agreed on a budget for LTCI, you now need to find the money for it. By repositioning the client's assets so that they work harder and produce more after-tax income, you can find funding.

Some clients have money they don't realize they could use. For instance, people with substantial assets in annuities may not think about tapping those funds. Most annuities, however, let you withdraw up to 10 percent of assets each year without penalty. Your client can use annual withdrawals to pay their LTCI premiums while the remaining money continues to grow, tax deferred. And if the annuity is a mediocre performer, you can do the client a favor by recommending that he exchange it for a better one. (However, there are other issues to consider and he may face surrender charges.)

Newer single-premium life policies that provide both a death benefit and living benefits for long-term care are another great solution that you should be aware of. Ask your client if he owns any paid-up life insurance. If so, the policy can be exchanged tax free under the Internal Revenue Code Sec. 1035 rule for a multipurpose life policy. (However, the client may face surrender charges.)

A wise advisor considers the cost of care and the client's available resources and finds a policy that is suitable for that particular client.

I've often spoken to people who were shown by another agent only a Cadillac policy they couldn't afford. When I show them a policy they can afford, they buy it.

People aren't aware of all the options they have when buying and funding LTCI. Knowing all the strategies and choices available makes you more valuable to your client. Be creative. When your client sees that you have his best interests at heart, you'll find that the LTCI sale is just the beginning of a mutually rewarding relationship.

Wilma Anderson is an LTCI sales trainer and producer in Littleton, Colo. Contact her at 720-344-0312 or at wilma@TheLTCcoach.com.

Have thorough knowledge of the long-term care insurance contract you are selling.

Too often, salespeople focus on the sizzle instead of the steak. But in selling LTCI, do not depend on just the sales brochures—read the contract. You need to know the contracts you are marketing well enough to show your prospects where a feature or benefit is described in the policy and to explain it clearly and concisely. Use the contract in conjunction with *A Shopper's Guide to Long-Term Care Insurance* to help your prospects understand how LTCI can preserve their assets and protect their loved ones.

Richard Weikart, CLU, ChFC, is a principal in Weikart
& Williams, a training design and development firm
in the Washington, D.C., area. You may reach him at
rweikart@comcast.net.

Take time to explore the client's emotional reasons for buying long-term care insurance.

Although each client will have different reasons, there are some trends to note. For example, for those over age 65, avoiding dependency is the reason they most often give for buying LTCI. They typically want to preserve their assets so they can take care of themselves and still have something left to leave to their heirs.

Men are more likely to buy an LTCI policy to protect their assets, while women are more likely to buy a policy to avoid becoming a burden to others. Younger buyers are more likely to be motivated by a desire to protect their retirement lifestyle by protecting their accumulated retirement assets.

Glenn E. Stevick Jr., CLU, ChFC, is an LUTC author and
editor. Contact him at glenns@amercoll.edu.
(Copyright © 2002 The American College. All rights
reserved. Used with permission.)

Learn to overcome long-term care insurance objections.

Anticipating and focusing on emotionally driven questions and objections are keys to successful LTCI sales. Being ready to address excuses with emotionally driven answers is the solution. Here are two examples.

Overcoming the excuse: "I'm so wealthy, I don't need it."

Trying to sell LTCI to wealthy people with a calculator in hand rarely works. Conversely, telling emotionally driven stories of clients in similar circumstances can be quite successful.

One such story is of a 60-year-old woman with assets valued at more than $1 million. Her interest income alone would have paid for the best quality care after retirement, without the need for her to ever deplete her principal. But her primary concern was with her family. Even though she had voluntarily made the choice to take in her own mother—and cared for her for six years without any regrets—she preferred not to have her grown children do the same for her. Purchasing LTCI assured her that she'd have peace of mind, and alleviated her fears of someday becoming a burden.

The initial approach that works best for the majority of prospects is to tell real-life stories. Getting people to take action is the dilemma. Helping them to anticipate the pain—making it real in their eyes—is the answer.

Counteracting the excuse: "I have a plan to call Dr. Kevorkian."

You could simply accept their plan at face value—to end life before long-term care becomes necessary. Or you could encourage them to continue this conversation by asking questions like, "What is your plan?" and "How will you know when the time is right?" You might challenge them further by asking, "Is the plan foolproof? Or could it unravel when you can no longer exercise control over your life?"

Here is an emotionally driven story to expose the fallibility of such plans: A man had instructed his son to "just shoot me" when the time came for long-term care. This went on for years—the father making the statement and the son agreeing.

Over the years, the father gradually lost his independence. First, he had heart problems and needed a nurse to come to the house a couple of times per week. When that happened, the father reminded the son about the plan to shoot him "if I get really bad." As the months passed, the father's condition worsened. When the son visited, the father kept reminding him of the plan.

Finally, it was too difficult for the father to live at home, and he had to move into a nursing home. Even when he entered into the long-term care environment, he still told his son, "If I get really bad and need care, just shoot me."

The bottom-line question is: Who's to decide when—exactly—things are so "bad" that life is no longer worth living?

When there's denial, there's no sense of logic involved. The key to this common objection from customers is to tell real-life stories. Then encourage the prospect to talk through his plan with you, allowing him the chance to talk himself out of it and recognize its flaws.

In the majority of cases, it's peace of mind that seals the deal. Helping people find their own versions of peace is the first step. With over two-thirds of consumers making these decisions using the emotional side of their brain, it's no wonder that financial advisors who rely primarily on logic to persuade prospects have a difficult time selling the product.

If you want to be successful in selling LTCI, sit back and listen. In that uncomfortable silence, your prospects will come to terms with the fact that their excuses are just a way to avoid taking action. When they

face that reality, they will then be open to hearing how they can move forward and more effectively take control of their lives.

> *Debra Newman is the founder and CEO of Newman Long Term Care and serves on AHIA's board of directors. You can reach her at* DebN@newmanLTC.com.

For better results selling long-term care insurance, use a one-minute sales presentation that goes something like this:

If you have reached the age of 65, you have a very good chance of making it to 85. If you are 85, there is a very high probability that you or someone close to you will be affected by the need for extended long-term health care.

The most serious long-term health care is residential nursing home care. In (your state), the average cost of this care is $X to $X a month, depending on care and location.

You can cover this cost in three ways:

1. You can write a monthly check out of your personal funds until your money is exhausted or reaches a certain minimum level.

2. Then you can go on welfare assistance through the state Medicaid program. The state reserves the right to decide where to place you for that care or

3. You can have a major insurance company pay all or the majority of the health-care costs through an LTCI policy.

LTCI is for those who would prefer No. 3.

*Stan Hustad is the leader of the PTM Group. Contact him
at 612-729-0420,* ptmark@aol.com *or through his website
at* www.ptmgroup.com.

When selling noncancellable long-term care insurance, add a COLA benefit.

When closing a noncancellable LTCI sale, the prospect frequently
objects to the premium, even though the benefit is paid monthly
to age 65. To illustrate the benefit fully and show the total benefit
paid to age 65 (assuming the prospect becomes disabled tomorrow), add a cost of living adjustment benefit. It will add up to millions of dollars and will easily justify the premium.

*Gerry Impelman, LUTCF, of Impelman Insurance Services
in San Antonio, Texas, can be reached at 210-340-088 or*
gerry@secure-benefits.com.

Learn about different care options and prices.

Thirteen-year LTCI veteran Honey Leveen suggests that advisors
visit as many assisted-living facilities as possible, and invest time learning about different care options and prices.

"My experience is that the public is hungry for knowledge about
where care is being given today and what their options will be," says
Leveen. "There's a general confusion about the kind of care Medicare
pays for and whether Medicare coverage duplicates LTCI coverage.
You need to be adept at describing the differences between nursing
homes, adult day care, personal care homes, assisted living, hospice
and independent living arrangements. An LTCI policy is often essentially a passport to access assisted living—which many potential clients
and even advisors may be still unaware of."

Don't sell nursing home insurance.

Jim Thornburgh, vice president of advanced sales at Innovative Solutions Insurance Services in Los Angeles, has this advice: "Don't say to a client, 'Here's some insurance in case you need to go to a nursing home.'"

Instead, he says, present LTCI products in terms of levels of care, which typically begin at home—the place where most people want to stay. Thornburgh suggests that you first show clients how the policy covers the cost of having someone go to the house to perform homemaking chores, therapy or food preparation. Then progress from there and say, "At some point, you may need round-the-clock help, and it may become cost-prohibitive to have someone come to your home. Even though it's not what you want now, you may need to move someday to some type of residential facility."

"Present it as a progression," advises Thornburgh. "'Buy this for when you need care at home; then if you need residential care someday, you'll have it.'"

Help clients afford coverage.

Long-term care insurance can be pricey. But if it is right for a client, a good advisor can help that client find a way to buy it.

"Prioritizing goals, giving a snapshot of a client's current objectives and financial condition, and recommending viable solutions is what I do every day," says Julie A. DeLiso, CFP, with MetLife Financial Services.

After she presented a seminar on long-term care, one couple expressed strong concern—and a desire to buy LTCI. But at first glance, it appeared to DeLiso that the husband, 67, and the wife, 50-something, couldn't afford the premium. Still, they were extremely motivated to buy and wanted a solution. So DeLiso began the financial-planning process and learned that the couple held a large mortgage with a balloon payment. After a comprehensive analysis of assets, she recommended that they refinance their home. The couple obtained a new mortgage, without the balloon payment, and freed up $700 a month—enough to cover the LTCI they needed.

(Reported by Lynn Vincent, contributor to Advisor Today)

Get involved.

As with any new product, you should begin the sales process by working with your existing clients. Steve Haas, CLU, FLMI, a State Farm agent in Bloomington, Ill., has built in a discussion of LTCI into his annual reviews and includes LTCI information as part of his routine client mailings.

As you develop your long-term care and LTCI skills, you should team up with someone who has more experience than you, advise both Peter Gelbwaks, CLTC, past president of the National Long-Term Care Network and president of Gelbwaks Insurance Services Inc., and Margie Barrie, a trainer, consultant and principal of LTCI Consulting Group, Inc.

You should also get a mentor and ask for home-office support. Partner with someone in your agency or team up with someone from your NAIFA chapter. Get to know the successful LTCI marketers in your area and learn what it takes to become one of them.

As you become comfortable with the basics of LTCI and develop a feel for working with prospects, consider the idea of specializing in the area. Become an expert and position yourself as the resource that other professionals can call on to address LTCI issues. As Arthea "Charlie" Reed, a Northwestern Mutual Financial Network representative in Asheville, N.C., points out, "You can't do retirement planning without discussing LTCI." So become the person who is positioned to

meet this specialized area of need. "Don't be an incidental producer," advises Gelbwaks. "Be a specialist. They don't just sell LTCI. They live and breathe it."

Richard Weikart, CLU, ChFC, is a principal in Weikart & Williams, a training design and development firm in the Washington, D.C., area. Contact him at rweikart@comcast.net.

If you're primarily involved in selling investments, don't forget to ask your clients about long-term care insurance protection.

More people would buy LTCI—but no one has ever asked them. It doesn't matter whether you make the annuity, the investment or the LTCI sale first. What's important is making that first sale and getting into a position to meet your clients' needs.

Wilma Anderson is an LTCI sales trainer and producer in Littleton, Colo. Contact her at 720-344-0312 or at wilma@TheLTCcoach.com.

Design the optimal long-term care insurance plan for your prospects and clients.

When you craft an LTCI plan that's designed to meet your clients' or prospects' needs and desires, you accomplish at least three things:

• You offer appropriate insurance protection the client can afford.

- You increase your closing rate markedly—and put yourself in position to turn a customer into a real client who will buy life insurance, annuities and mutual funds from you.

- Because you provided a plan that meets their needs, your happy new clients will gladly refer you to their friends. It's a win-win situation for all.

People in different age brackets and circumstances have different needs and respond to different features—both from an emotional and a rational point of view. And while some clients may have some idea about the policy features they want, most don't. So you can't simply ask, "What would you like?" You need to take the lead.

A plan for younger clients

While LTCI is still mostly bought by the 65-plus crowd, more people in their early 60s, 50s and even 40s are concerned about their financial risk for long-term care. Educate them that the safest choice is to buy insurance now, while their health is good and they can still health-qualify for insurance.

For your prospects in their 40s or early 50s, it's a more challenging sale because they don't see an immediate need. So ask about their parents and grandparents. How long did they live? Are any still living? Have they needed care? This will help make the issue more real to them—especially if their relatives tend to live to a ripe old age.

Because the base premium is much lower for younger clients than it is for people in their 70s, your clients and prospects can afford a feature-rich policy. Some valuable features add surprisingly little cost, and one of the most important is an unlimited benefit period. At younger issue ages, the difference in cost between a three-year benefit and an unlimited benefit is minimal, so always recommend the latter.

You can point out that while the odds are that they'll use their benefits in their old age, anything can happen to anyone at anytime. Healthy people can be struck down by an accident at any age, and the incidence of chronic diseases such as multiple sclerosis and Parkinson's disease rises sharply for people in their 50s. Your clients won't want to run out of benefits, especially if they're going to live another 20, 30 or more years. Also, people who have a limited policy might be afraid to start using their benefits because they feel they have to save them for later. That's not a good position to be in.

Another crucial feature for younger buyers is compound inflation protection. A typical plan offers 5 percent, compounded annually. Another option indexes benefit increases to the Consumer Price Index. Inflation protection is a must because it's impossible to predict what care might cost 20 or 30 years from now. I normally add a compound-inflation rider for buyers up to age 65.

Having no elimination period (0 days) is also well worth obtaining, and is affordable at younger ages. Again, the goal is risk control. Many years from now, 30 or 60 or more days of care will be very expensive.

Younger buyers often have this objection: "What if I pay premiums for years and never use the insurance?" Remind them that they may have paid premiums on their auto insurance for lots of years, too. It's all about peace of mind when they have a claim and start receiving long-term care insurance benefits. Another alternative is to show them the return-of-premium rider. If the insured has not used any benefits before his or her death, the insurer will return a portion of the premium to the beneficiary. The rider is available only on policies purchased by age 65.

A survivorship benefit is attractive to couples. This option will pay the surviving spouse's premiums for the rest of her life, as long as she has owned the policy for 10 years and has not made any claims.

The rider must be purchased before age 65 and typically costs just 5 percent extra. Some insurers include the feature automatically in all newly issued policies.

With younger buyers, discuss a 10-pay policy that's fully paid up after 10 years. A 55-year-old, for example, can buy the policy and be done paying premiums by normal retirement age. It's also an appealing feature for business owners because LTCI premiums are now 100 percent deductible as a business expense. The benefit doesn't have to be offered to all employees; it can be carved out for just the owner, and, if desired, key managers.

Age 66 to early 70s
Plan design here involves a balancing act between desirable features and available funds. While an unlimited benefit period with full inflation protection is ideal, past the age of 65, these features start to cost considerably more.

I usually recommend simple inflation protection for this age bracket. Since clients in this age group will probably be using their benefits within 10 to 15 years, simple inflation provides adequate protection at a lower cost than a compound inflation feature. (Some states do not allow simple inflation, only a compound inflation rider, so be sure to check before offering this to a client.)

Another reasonable compromise is a shorter benefit period because an unlimited benefit can add considerable expense to their budget at this age. On average, men choose a three-year benefit, while women, who expect to outlive their husbands and want to ensure they're taken care of, prefer unlimited benefits. However, men who come from long-lived families may want to get unlimited coverage. It's best to illustrate different benefit periods and let your clients choose. By giving them options, you make them feel that they don't need to shop around and talk to another agent.

The restoration of benefits rider is a valuable feature for people who select a limited benefit period. This means that if the insured starts collecting benefits, then recovers and is treatment-free for at least six months, the policy benefits will be restored to the original provision when it was issued. Some policies from the large carriers include this automatically; some charge about 5 percent extra for it.

Mid-70s and beyond

People in this age group are the most ready to buy LTCI. They realize they must make a decision before their health declines and they can't get insurance.

However, higher premiums for this group can cause sticker shock. Older clients can save money by declining inflation protection. Since they're likely to use their benefits relatively soon, this isn't too risky, provided they start out with a higher daily benefit, such as $200 to $300 a day. Again, illustrate both limited-pay plans and unlimited benefit periods, show the costs with and without the inflation rider, and help the client make a good decision.

Suggesting a long elimination period, though, can backfire. For example, a 90-day elimination period may save money up front, but it's risky. If another agent has suggested a 90-day period, you might ask, "Did the other agent tell you that if Medicare doesn't pay for any long-term care benefits, you could have a $15,000 deductible today? (90 days x $167 per day in a nursing home = $ 15,000)" And point out that health-care costs are sure to go up.

With a lower elimination period, the client would have to pay for 20 or 30 days out-of-pocket if Medicare does not pay for anything. To self-insure that deductible, your clients can use annuities (fixed-rate or equity-indexed) to help their money work harder, tax-deferred.

Wilma Anderson is an LTCI sales trainer and producer in Littleton, Colo. Contact her at 720-344-0312 or at wilma@TheLTCcoach.com.

Learn the secrets of long-term care insurance sales success.

In my 14 years in the long-term care insurance industry, I have found that the question insurance agents ask the most is this: "What are your secrets for succeeding in LTCI sales?"

The answer is simple: Be active, dial and smile, and above all, believe in the product.

Successful salespeople know that a solid sale often requires a transfer of beliefs from the agent to the prospect. I always take my own LTCI policy on sales interviews and show it to prospects. Some agents who have family members in care situations take copies of the monthly invoices for their loved ones' care. Recently, after seeing a $5,500 nursing-home bill for one month of care for one agent's father, a prospect did not hesitate to apply for private LTCI. Seeing really is believing.

See the country.

Another idea that has worked well for me is telling people who already know I sell insurance that I am actually in the "motor home" business. Few people want to talk about the possibility that they may need long-term care, but because they know I sell insurance, they're quite inquisitive about my being in the motor home business.

Most people in the LTCI marketing "sweet spot" have an emergency fund set aside, "just in case" unforeseen circumstances arise. In many cases, these standby funds have grown considerably because they have been left alone to grow—just in case.

"In case of what?" I ask. I often hear, "In case we get sick," or some similar response. I help them realize that their special fund is actually there to help fund long-term care expenses. I show them that transferring a portion of the risk of potentially high long-term care expenses away from their own assets to a reliable insurance company, however, can free their special fund to—you guessed it—buy a motor home and see the country.

Build an island cabin.

I had a similar sales scenario in Seattle. The husband of a couple I was interviewing had recently retired from his service manager's position at a local car dealership, but the wife was still teaching. Why wasn't she retired? They wanted to be sure they had enough money tucked away "just in case." This couple's rainy-day fund was just over $30,000.

In addition to their Seattle home, the couple had a one-acre lakefront lot on Orcas Island in the San Juan Islands. The husband had purchased the property years before with the idea of building a cabin on the lake and enjoying peace and solitude in their retirement years. They had never built their cabin. I asked them how much it might cost to build a cabin, and the husband indicated between $20,000 and $25,000. I asked why they hadn't used part of their rainy-day fund to build it. They finally admitted they were afraid the husband might have a heart attack or possibly a stroke, as his brother had.

When I showed them an LTCI policy that worked with their budget and provided protection in excess of the amount they'd accumulated in their rainy-day fund, they applied immediately. A week after their policies were delivered, I received a telephone call from the wife. "You'll never guess what we've done," she said. "We've started to build our cabin on Orcas Island, and I have submitted my retirement request to the school board."

That was eight years ago. Were it not for my determining this couple's hot buttons, learning what their concerns were and providing them with some solutions that would help them do what they wanted to do in life, she would probably still be teaching, and he would still be sitting around their Seattle home reading. There would be no cabin on Orcas Island, now a haven for them as well as their three children and seven grandchildren.

The bottom line

Talk to people. Find out what's important to them. Develop an acceptable, affordable solution to their potential long-term care needs and show them how it can help them achieve one or more of their wants. Then take advantage of the contagious nature of this product and ask for referrals.

There are literally millions of aging Baby Boomers who don't yet have this important form of protection. The opportunities are there. Good luck!

Bob Callanan, LTCP, is a regional sales manager for GE Financial Assurance. He may be reached by email at bob. callanan@ge.com.

MULTILINE

Use boat owners insurance as a door opener.

Do you love boating or do you own your own boat? If you are a multiline agent, market boat-owners insurance as a door opener, then move to life, disability income and health insurance. Most boat owners have high incomes, along with tax and estate problems. As a fellow boat owner, you speak their lingo. Get the first appointment on their boat. It works.

Lawrence Fowler Jr., CLU, LUTCF, is a member of the NAIFA Board of Trustees and an agent with L. Fowler Insurance Agency, Nationwide Insurance and Financial. You may reach him at 860-889-7740.

Go high-tech.

In the late 1800s, Chas A. Tegner, a Swedish immigrant, hit it big in the Alaskan gold rush. Then in 1902, he used his windfall to open a small insurance agency in Santa Monica, Calif. Tegner, and later his son and daughters, ran the family business for more than six decades. Today, Tegner-Miller Insurance is the oldest business in town.

But old doesn't mean old-fashioned. In fact, the $33 million, 39-employee firm is on the cutting edge of technology. In the mid-1980s, Tegner-Miller used an IBM mainframe that Aetna had given it to install its first computerized agency-management system. In 1994, when most people were still muttering "http ... what?" the firm launched its first website. Today, Tegner-Miller is engaged in a continuous, technology-based quest for improvement. You can visit the firm's website at *www.tmib.com.*

"We undergo constant quality improvement and process improvement," says principal Bill Aspinwall. "We've made every effort to integrate technology into our operations. That's critical for multiline because you have so many different things you're doing all day long. Technology helps us manage it all efficiently."

Just one example: Tegner-Miller runs, in addition to its main website, four niche websites. Three sites target specific insurance needs, but only one need per site: earthquake coverage, auto insurance and medical malpractice coverage. A fourth site targets a specific customer segment: business managers employed by Hollywood entertainers.

Using this niche approach, Tegner-Miller sells one or two policies a week online and gathers another 50 telephone inquiries from prospects who are unable to qualify through its online, direct-rater process. Advisors close another four to five of those prospects each week.

Aspinwall increases site success by renting key words from Overture, an Internet marketing service. That helps Tegner-Miller's sites rank high in premiere Internet search engines such as Yahoo.

The agency's commitment to technology extends from high-end endeavors to more mundane daily functions such as fax management. Tegner-Miller's fax traffic is so heavy, Aspinwall says, that the firm once employed a person whose job consisted solely of sorting through incoming paper faxes and running them to various offices. So the firm decided to automate.

Today, every fax is sent and received via a desktop computer, with incoming faxes routed by the receptionist over the office network. As a result, the agency saves time and money: no more hunting down lost faxes, since they're all stored on the network. There is also no need for a full-time fax-runner; that individual was redeployed to more productive administrative duties.

Aspinwall considers such technological tweaking essential to a successful multiline practice. "I'm managing personal, commercial, benefits, estate planning, the whole thing. The only way I can stay on top of it all is to have everything on my desktop."

(Reported by Lynn Vincent, contributor to Advisor Today)

Form strategic partnerships.

Gary West is president of Texas BancPartners, an independent insurance agency partly owned by Oaks Bank and Trust Co. and Lone Star Bank, which are community banks in the Dallas area. Though West's agency had always done some group and life insurance business with property and casualty (P/C) customers, the income derived from those products was never more than 10 percent of the company's annual total commission revenues. West expects this percentage to more than double this year because the firm recently formed a strategic alliance with IPS Advisors, a large life insurance and benefits agency that offers a wide range of variable insurance products and estate-planning options. Texas BancPartners is currently educating bank officers about identifying good prospects for these products, too.

West, a 30-year veteran of P/C sales, says he's amazed at the depth of the relationships banks have with their customers. "There's a trusted advisor relationship there that's incredible," he says. "In the community banking world, customers follow their bankers everywhere. That's the kind of relationship we're trying to create, and it's working. We think it's going to work on the financial side."

(Reported by Julie Crawshaw, contributor to Advisor Today)

Offer new partners lucrative opportunities.

When shopping for partners or associates with another specialty, you should try to offer them financially attractive commission splits if you want high-quality expertise. This is according to Andy Muma, CIC, LIC, vice president and sales manager of Hudson & Muma in Royal Oak, Mich. Writing coverage for specialized property and casualty needs like film production, weddings and aviation gave Muma great respect for people with specialized knowledge. So when the agency decided to add life and group health insurance, it offered a very generous commission share to get two excellent life specialists they found through extensive networking.

It was a smart move. The new associates quickly built life and annuity product sales to 30 percent of the firm's overall revenues. Years later, after one of the original life specialists left and the other died, Hudson & Muma partnered with a life specialist agency to form Financial Guardian, LLC. "We're all under one roof and refer business to each other," Muma says, "but everyone sticks to his own line of work."

(Reported by Julie Crawshaw, contributor to Advisor Today*)*

Find a good back-office provider.

Efficiency and access to top carriers should be a priority if you want to start selling life and health insurance products in today's competitive and difficult insurance market, notes John Dawson, CEO of Financial Keyosk. Yet the current market environment makes getting contracts with top companies all but impossible.

One solution is to use a reputable vendor who works with independent agents and provides the necessary contracts and technology. The most comprehensive of these firms offer aspiring life and health agents a completely Web-accessible back office with a database for tracking customers, two types of forms (for experts and beginners) and highly automated processes.

You should not rely solely on this technology to achieve results, however. It is widely known that pure Internet marketing hasn't worked because it lacks a personal component. Instead, Dawson advocates using the Internet only as a facilitator of communications and for transfer of data—not to get new customers.

(Reported by Julie Crawshaw, contributor to Advisor Today*)*

Here is what to do if you have insurance burnout.

We in the multiline business have a tremendous opportunity for life, health and related sales. However, by the time we are finished with the homeowners, auto or business proposals, everyone is usually exhausted and suffering from insurance burnout. My tip to any multiline agent is to close your manuals and sell the next appointment at that time.

Most of the factfinding has already been done so that very little additional information will be needed. The next day, you can follow up with a nice thank-you note and confirm your next appointment in writing.

Laura DeLauder Haraway, LUTCF, is with the DeLauder Insurance Agency in Maryland. You may reach her at 301-694-0028.

Target market your product.

A good sales idea for the mutliline agent is to determine your most competitive product and target market that product.

For example, if you are strong in contractor's liability, join associations related to that industry. And remember that givers gain. There is more satisfaction in giving than just being on the take. Whenever possible, refer your customers to members of that association.

Lee Walters, LUTCF, is with the American National Life Insurance Co. in California. You may reach him at 805-544-4515, lee@ljwinsurance.com.

Learn how to retain your life insurance business.

When it comes to retaining their life business, successful agencies share several common characteristics. Here are some tips you can use to build your insurance and financial services practice.

Tip #1: Sell it right the first time. All professionals know that you want to sell your client the right way the first time so that you can form a long-term relationship based on value and trust. Successful multiline agencies sell life insurance products in a process that consists of two or more steps. They know that you do not want to sell on the first appointment because doing so is almost always based strictly on emotion. Policies that stay on the books are sold with both logic and emotion. This means proper factfinding and a thoughtful follow-up presentation, which will enable you to fill your customer's needs. Needs-based selling has always shown a better persistency than other types of selling and lays the groundwork for future sales.

Tip #2: After the life policy is sold, professionals recommend a follow-up call to the client in less than 30 days to avoid loss of the sale due to buyer's remorse. Reselling the policy while memories are fresh helps cement the sale and reminds the customer about what a good decision he has made. This call also continues the "building-the-relationship" process.

Tip #3: Put a reminder on your calendar to follow up again on the fourth month of the anniversary of the sale. Many studies have been done to support this action. If a policy is going to lapse in the first year, the pros will tell you it will happen in the first three to four months. This follow-up call further distinguishes your sales approach from the typical monoline sales approach of "sell 'em and forget 'em."

Tip #4: Have a formal review program. All successful insurance practitioners have identified a way to meet with their clients at least once a year. This is a must if you plan on being successful in creating a local insurance and financial services superstore™. The review should not be used as a selling tool but as another opportunity to resell your client and uncover unmet needs. It is the only way for the multiline agent to guarantee that he is keeping this very important promise to his clients.

Tip #5: Touch the customer. Relationships need to be nourished. I have never had a client tell me that I gave him too much time and attention. If you want your customer relationships to flourish, keep in touch. This can be done through a phone call, simple hand-written notes or programmed letters to keep your agency and your company's brand name in front of your policyholders. With technology today and support from company marketing departments, it has never been easier to keep in touch with our very valuable clients. Sending out birthday cards and newsletters is still a very effective way to stay connected. Whatever method you chose, put a system in place that provides a consistent program to stay connected with your customers.

In business, retention is everything. Retaining customers is not only profitable, it is also a solid foundation that guarantees future growth. In 20 years of practicing in the insurance field, I have found that my clients' needs change about every three years. This means that everyone who has purchased life insurance from me is going to need more insurance in the not-too-distant future.

By retaining my customers, I also block out competitors who have products that are more price sensitive. Rounding out the account with additional lines of insurance and then wrapping it up with good retention strategies is just one more way for the multiline agency to grow into the future.

Troy Korsgaden has twice been named "Agent of the Year" from among 14,000 Farmers Insurance agents. He has trained nearly 40,000 insurance agents and staff. For more information, call 800-524-6390, fax the company at 559-625-4990 or go to www.tksystems.org.

NICHE MARKETS—
WOMEN, SENIORS AND MINORITIES

Don't treat women like men.

Women write 80 percent of all checks—both corporate and personal—and make 81 percent of all purchase decisions about products and services. Maybe it's time for you to begin targeting your sales to them.

To do this, however, you need to update your marketing and sales tactics. Women continue to be sold to as if they were men. To successfully sell to women, you need to understand and address some important facts:

Women are relationship-oriented. They see relationships as fundamental to the buying process. You must be willing to establish and nurture long-lasting relationships with your female clients. This is in contrast to men, who are often less loyal in their purchasing habits. Many women fear that they will outlive their assets and are looking for an advisor they can trust and with whom they can establish a long-term relationship.

Women seek advice and education. Education is key to attracting more women clients. According to LIMRA International, only 50 percent of women consider themselves fairly to very knowledgeable about investments, compared to 75 percent of men. However, women—unlike men—are willing to admit they need advice and will look to a financial advisor for that help. They are more open to learning than men. Therefore seminars are a powerful tool.

A longer sales process is normal. Women and men go through the buying process differently. In general, men are transactional buyers, making their decisions based on facts, logic and hierarchy. They also make their purchasing decisions more quickly than women do. Women, however, want the facts before they buy and take their time in assessing what the advisor is offering. So, it is important to educate them, wait as they take their time with the decision and return at a later date to close the sale.

(Reported by Maggie Leyes, Managing Editor of Advisor Today, *based on the Marketing Financial Products and Services to Women conference sponsored by the Institute for International Research)*

Appreciate gender differences.

The time is right to multiply your sales with the people who buy the most—women. Women as a whole are a powerful buying source. Women are brand loyal. Eighty-six percent of businesswomen will use the same products and services at home as they do in their businesses for familiarity and convenience.

So how do you increase your sales among women? First you must appreciate the gender differences in the purchasing process. Once you understand that the sales process is different for women than for men, and that the process will take more patience and may take you twice the amount of time to close the first sale, then you've taken the first step toward increasing your market share.

Keep in mind that women are brand loyal, so they will continue to give you their business. Men on the other hand will purchase from multiple companies. In short, your long-term return on investment is greater with women clients.

Delia Passi is an expert and sales trainer on marketing and selling financial services to women and multicultural markets. Contact her at 305-918-0750 or delia@medelia.com.

Transfer widows' IRAs.

Many widows have large individual retirement accounts they are "saving" for beneficiaries. They don't realize that much of the IRA will be lost to income taxation. The solution is a capital transfer of all or part of the IRA for life insurance to preserve and enhance the wealth passed to beneficiaries.

Donna K. Nearhood, J.D., CLU, ChFC, is the affluent markets consultant for Columbus Life Insurance Co. in Cincinnati. Contact her at 800-677-8383 or at Donna. Nearhood@columbuslife.com.

Learn how to communicate with women.

Here are some pointers on how to communicate with women throughout the sales process:

Let women take the lead. Women are information gatherers and do not want you to "fix" their situation by providing quick solutions. They want to make educated decisions by asking a lot of questions. When dealing with a female prospect, taking time to answer her questions in detail will provide her with the comfort level she seeks to make purchasing decisions.

Keep up with them. Women communicate differently than men and may tell you stories so that they feel comfortable that they've relayed their messages to you. This may seem like scattered thinking, when in actuality they are further into the decision process than you might think. So while you are thinking your prospect can't stay focused, she's probably wondering why you can't keep up.

Don't push the close. Women will purchase when they're satisfied they are making the best decision. This means multiple factors come into play such as: How will this decision affect my family? Is the advisor to be trusted? What is the company's reputation? Can I trust that this product will serve all my needs?

Build a relationship. Women value relationships and will be prone to trust you if they feel you are equally interested in creating a long-term relationship. That's easier said than done, but if you strive to build a long-term relationship, your efforts will be rewarded by her dollars, loyalty and referrals.

Delia Passi is an expert and sales trainer on marketing and selling financial services to women and multicultural markets. Contact her at 305-918-0750 or delia@medelia.com.

Market to women on a career track.
Women on a career track have become an important economic force and play a substantial part in family financial decision making.

Long-term care insurance is an important and timely product for women. However, women's needs may vary depending on age, life stage, income, whether they own their own business or work for someone else, and if they have responsibility for family members.

I suggest gathering information on current clients, conducting educational/informational seminars, and participating in women's organizations. Ask questions to get a complete picture. Offer other product options when appropriate. For example, propose disability income insurance for women in their income-earning years.

*Pam Delaney is vice president and chief operating officer at
MassMutual Financial Group. For further information, visit*
www.notaburden.com *and* www.halfapaycheck.com.

Sell a buy/sell agreement funded with life insurance to female business owners.

There are more than 9 million women-owned businesses in the
United States, generating $3.6 trillion in annual revenues. Fewer than
26 percent of them have a funded, business-succession plan. A buy/
sell agreement funded with life insurance ensures continuation of the
business beyond the owner's lifetime.

*Donna K. Nearhood, J.D., CLU, ChFC, is the affluent
markets consultant for Columbus Life Insurance Co. in
Cincinnati. Contact her at 800-677-8383 or at* Donna.
Nearhood@columbuslife.com.

Value cultural differences.

The Hispanic consumer market is growing much more rapidly than
the non-Hispanic market in the United States. To increase your sales
among this fast-growing market segment, you should value their cultural differences. One way to do this is to be sensitive to your office
set up. Hispanic people tend to involve more family members when
making decisions that will affect the family. So a typical sales call may
involve the spouse, parents and possibly older children or other close
relatives. To accommodate them, make sure there is adequate space
for a large family in your office or wherever you meet. One or two
chairs will not be enough.

*Delia Passi is an expert and sales trainer on marketing and
selling financial services to women and multicultural markets. Contact her at 305-918-0750 or* delia@medelia.com.

Respond to cultural differences in Asian-American subgroups.

While the term "Asian American" provides a convenient way to
describe the market as a whole, marketers have found that success
comes from targeting key segments within the Asian-American
market share. You can do so by marketing and selling to large,
higher-income population segments, primarily Koreans, Chinese,
Vietnamese, Filipinos, Japanese and South Asians.

Responding to their cultural differences in their purchasing process
is equally important. For example, Asian Americans in general are
detail-oriented and expect to have a substantial amount of information
early in the sales process.

*Delia Passi is an expert and sales trainer on marketing and
selling financial services to women and multicultural markets. Contact her at 305-918-0750 or* delia@medelia.com.

Here are some key issues to understand before tackling the Chinese-American market.

Chinese Americans, in general, are highly educated, earn high
incomes and are concerned about financial preparation to care for
themselves and their extended families. All of these are qualities that
facilitate the sale of insurance.

Interestingly, however, a LIMRA study, *Marketing to Chinese Americans*, showed that fewer than half of the Chinese-American study respondents own individual life insurance.

The stumbling block to ownership can be attributed to a number of factors. Many find it difficult to decide what type of insurance to buy, and whether to buy it from an agent or through a company. In addition, 40 percent of the respondents admitted not knowing the importance of life insurance, and an additional 30 percent felt that their group coverage from work was adequate. The good news: Cost was not a factor; only 10 percent felt insurance was too expensive.

This data belies Chinese Americans' concern about dying without protecting their loved ones—some 60 percent felt "somewhat or very concerned." In a culture that emphasizes the extended family, insurance becomes a critical financial-planning tool for family heads to address their concerns about caring for both children and their elderly parents. The study highlights a number of financial goals that are important to Chinese Americans, including retirement planning, their children's education and caring for aging parents.

These facts open up an attractive avenue for advisors to bring their financial-planning knowledge and a suite of products to bear in solving this group's financial dilemmas. Advisors interested in approaching this market should understand a few salient points from this study:

- Chinese Americans view saving as important, so advisors should emphasize permanent life insurance vs. term insurance as well as annuities.

- Higher education is paramount (70 percent of parents were concerned about how to pay for it), so offering products to help families plan and save for their higher-education goals is critical.

- Advisors who work with a well-known company have an advantage in this market, as an overwhelming majority of Chinese Americans think brand is important, and "regard a company's financial stability and reputation as extremely important."

- The use of translated marketing/educational information and having an agent who speaks Chinese (Mandarin or Cantonese) are important factors in reaching first-generation prospects.

- Chinese Americans, especially first-generation, may not be aware that insurance agents can also provide complete financial-planning products and services.

Nine U.S. cities hold significant Chinese-American populations—Los Angeles, San Francisco, Seattle, New York, Boston, Washington D.C., Chicago, Houston and Atlanta—and represent strong opportunities for advisors interested in tapping this market.

(Reported by Maggie Leyes, Managing Editor of Advisor Today)

Remember these tips if you want to be successful in selling to seniors:

- The lifetime income annuity is gaining popularity among them because their No. 1 concern is outliving their assets.

- Confidence about what you're selling is important. Seniors can tell when you don't really know what you're talking about.

- It doesn't work to try to impress seniors with technical terms. You'll lose them.

- Seniors want to be shown evidence, such as an article from *The Wall Street Journal.*

- Seniors love seminars. The most popular topics are tax reduction, increasing retirement income, distributions from individual retirement accounts, and long-term care insurance.

- Working with seniors means accommodating their physical needs, including having your offices on the ground floor, making parking easy and having a small, round meeting table to simulate the coziness of a kitchen table.

- Seniors are not optimizers; they are "satisfiers." The best recommendation for selling to them is getting a synthesis of the right technical advice, and the advice they will feel good in accepting. Seniors are especially averse to new money ideas. If you must introduce an innovation, relate it to something they are already familiar with.

- Big is better. Seniors trust large, well-known institutions and authorities. If you work for a lesser-known firm or have your own practice, you may start out at a disadvantage. You will need to create the same level of comfort that your senior prospect has when he's working with a household name. Do this by educating your prospect about the advantages of doing business with you.

- Asset protection is a priority. If you want to win in the senior market, make sure the foundation of your communication is about asset protection, reducing risk, diversification, safety, protecting the nest egg, leaving something to the grandkids and having a comfortable lifestyle.

- Earn their trust. Seniors will not do business with an advisor they do not trust. Fortunately, creating trust with seniors is not about possessing credentials, degrees or even a great investment track record. It is all about what you do.

(Reported by Chuck Jones, former senior editor of Advisor Today*)*

Follow these words of wisdom and you will be able to build trust quickly with seniors.

- Never use jargon. Each time you use a term your prospect doesn't understand, you reduce your chances for success.

- Know your craft. If you don't have the knowledge you need, take classes or train yourself. Knowledge includes technical and product expertise.

- Answer their questions clearly. Let them finish asking the question, repeat it to them to ensure that you understood it, and then answer. Remember that the question you think they might ask is not necessarily what they will ask. Listen, repeat and answer.

- Do what you say you will do. Be on time, send the promised item and call when you said you would. Your word must be meticulously maintained or seniors will not do business with you.

Larry Klein, CPA, is a Certified Senior Advisor and heads NF Communications in Walnut Creek, Calif. Contact him through his website, www.nfcom.com.

Here are additional tips for achieving success in the senior market.

- Sell insurance as a way to protect assets. If it is a struggle for your client to find money to pay for coverage, he probably does not have enough assets to protect and would not be a good candidate for some types of coverage.

- People in their retirement years, many seniors, typically buy four types of insurance, each with a specific purpose:

  1. Maximum-funded life insurance, typically as a single premium, for the purpose of accumulating tax-free cash value

  2. Survivorship life—to reduce and pay estate taxes

  3. Annuities, because they are tax-deferred and provide an income

  4. Long-term care insurance

- Provide a lot of personal service. Most seniors do not like calling up only to talk to a machine.

- Sell yourself, not the product.

- Do not use high-pressure sales tactics. You cannot go too slowly in a sales interview.

- To find money for insurance, look for assets to transfer, such as money in certificates of deposit or in pension rollovers.

- The money seniors have was earned at a rate well below today's salaries.

- A few hundred dollars constitute a great deal of money to most seniors.

- If possible, contact senior prospects by calling on their adult children.

- If possible, contact elderly prospects through a referral or a third-party endorsement.

- Get both the husband and wife involved in the sale even though the majority of sales are made with the husband.

(Reported in Advisor Today)

Realize that the buying methods of people aged 65 and older are different from those under 65.

According to Jim Hall, a professor with the department of psychiatry and human behavior at the University of North Texas, the products seniors want to buy are usually based on their life experiences. So getting to know them is vital. Discipline, self-denial, doing something on behalf of others, compassion, altruism and personal privacy are a few of the dominant values displayed by the mature market.

Most seniors were influenced by the Great Depression and World War II, and the serious financial and social outcomes of these events have, and will, influence the way they ultimately buy. They like to make judgements based on their intuition and do not like to be manipulated, coerced or controlled.

Remember, too, that not all people 65 or older are the same. Some may be "old" as measured by their physical or cognitive abilities, but others, older than 85, are comparatively young by the same measurements. They also do not like to be thought of as old. They prefer to be reflected in an attractive and positive fashion.

Relationships are the most important asset of both the business and the salesperson, and there is a real difference between relationship marketing and relationship selling. Relationship marketing is the never-ending process of improving the linkages between a company, its prospects and its customers or clients, resulting in greater value. Relationship selling is the one-on-one association between a customer and a salesperson. It involves the salesperson adding value by developing a personal and business connection with the customer.

Seniors can be quite leery of almost everyone. They may see an individual with whom they have not established a relationship as encroaching on their personal space. The following are keys to developing a relationship in which the senior is comfortable and receptive to a message. When communicating with a senior:

- Convey respect.

- Be patient.

- Watch and listen for impairments such as mental, cognitive, hearing and visual impairments. Pace your presentation to deal with any of these impairments.

- Always confirm appointments with the senior. A reminder postcard is preferable to a phone call. A telephone reminder gives the senior an opportunity to cancel while the postcard requires him to be proactive in order to cancel the appointment.

Comfort, security and safety are key psychological needs. And convenience and access may be as important as the product itself.

Edwin J. Pittock, Certified Senior Advisor, trains financial advisors and others in the ins and outs of doing business with older clients. He is based in Denver and can be reached at 800-653-1785.

Use a newsletter to get in front of your mature prospects and clients.

According to the Pew Research Center on the People and the Press, newspapers are still the preferred information source for the 50-plus crowd, and they spend an average of 23 minutes each day reading newspapers, compared to an average of 11 minutes each day for younger segments. An obvious but often overlooked approach is to make a news-based informational newsletter your direct-mail vehicle.

An informational newsletter covers a variety of useful information not only about your product or service, but also about other life issues of importance, such as health, legal, Social Security and housing issues. In some of the newsletters we produce for mature consumers, we'll include as many as eight different topic areas.

By using a combination of information and motivation, you can do more than just get your 15 seconds of attention. You can actually build a relationship with your client and prospect. A sponsored monthly, bimonthly or quarterly newsletter gets you in front of your audience on a regular basis as a resource that responds to their questions, needs and concerns, at about the same cost as a traditional direct-mail piece. Newsletters can cost just a few dollars per year plus postage, often less than the cost of one slick direct-mail piece.

Here are five ways a newsletter-based direct-mail approach can benefit you as well as your mature clients and prospects:

1. Newsletters keep your clients and prospects focused on your message. This is one of the great advantages of direct mail in general. If you're in a card pack, however, your prospects may be receiving four to six solicitations at the same time for the same product you're offering. A newsletter allows you to control what and from whom your customer will get information and focuses them on you and your message.

2. A newsletter establishes credibility. You can highlight your company's expertise and competence through articles you write and by providing information from your partner organizations, CPAs, elder-law attorneys, care managers, etc.

3. Newsletters take advantage of the mental and behavioral conditioning created as people process information. We often create an "information sandwich." By starting out with "news" on a topic of interest, readers get conditioned to processing that type of information. We then include information about the company, product, services, etc., and follow up with more news and factual content. In this way, your promotional message gets processed as "news," and is more likely to be absorbed intellectually.

4. A newsletter reinforces your value without being a relentless "infomercial." Repetition is a key to effective advertising and promotion, and, most importantly, establishing a relationship with your clients and prospects. But that's the one thing usually missing from the typical, one-shot, direct-mail approach, to which only 0.1 percent to

3 percent of consumers respond immediately. What about the other 97 percent to 99.9 percent?

A periodic newsletter is a very cost-efficient way to get in front of all your potential customers repeatedly. In addition, informational newsletters typically have a 25 percent to 50 percent "pass-along" rate. The addressee, as well as spouse, friends and neighbors, is often in the reader loop.

5. Newsletters can provide an interactive connection. Just because a newsletter is informational doesn't mean it can't include a response to you or another call to action. In fact, it should have all the power of a traditional direct-mail solicitation, but in a "soft-sell," information-based package. You can offer free consultations, additional brochures and informational seminars through a well-designed and well-prepared newsletter just as you would with any direct-mail piece.

Here's one caution: In all your marketing communications to seniors, make sure that you use font sizes, colors, styles, graphic design and cultural references that will make the message easy for this group to read and understand.

John Migliaccio, Ph.D., RFG, is president of the American Institute of Financial Gerontology and author of 77 Truths About Marketing to the 50+ Consumer. *For more information, visit* www.aifg.org. *or call 888-367-8470.*

ODDS AND ENDS

TECHNOLOGY

Use online tools to sell voluntary benefits.

In the voluntary benefits marketplace, effectively weaving Web resources into traditional business practices can accelerate sales growth without the need to abandon the classic sales approach. Whether you are servicing existing clients or proposing or selling insurance to prospects, Internet-based tools can pave alternate routes for your prospects and drive decisions at the customer level.

As a financial advisor, you must raise your clients' awareness of your products and services and establish a need for them. In your drive to accomplish this objective, you are always looking for new sales ideas to help enhance your clients' buying experiences.

To achieve success when integrating Web components into traditional sales methods, you must first identify integration points whereby Internet-based advances can improve communications, needs assessment, application, sales tracking and administration.

You can become more effective in the sales and education process by leveraging well-known Internet features. These include "customizability" for needs assessment, "interactivity" for enabling online application, and 24/7 "availability" for delivering convenience to your prospects and empowering family decisions.

What's more, by integrating online services into the sales process, you can easily differentiate your product from that of your competitors while enriching the company's voluntary benefits offerings and providing a cost-effective and time-efficient solution to the employer's administrative problems. Thanks to online functionality, voluntary benefit cases are now being placed within as little as a month after meetings with employees, regardless of the type of insurance product sold.

If you're thinking of interchanging traditional sales techniques with an Internet-based approach, here are effective strategies that will help accelerate your sales:

Depending on what you use when navigating the information superhighway, you will find educational websites with links to questions and answers for your prospects, automated shows for further illustration, interactive needs calculators to help them meet their personal needs, dynamic savings evaluators, hyperlinked glossaries and streaming video testimonials.

To further your online communications efforts with your prospects, consider performing an "e-census." You can do this by targeting the decision makers or owners of companies that have a propensity toward the use of technology, such as firms in business service industries. At the same time, you should continue to focus on companies with which you have developed a strong relationship, where there are ties to other benefits, and where you have an opportunity to learn about ways to enhance existing plans.

Keep in mind that there are always cost-effective opportunities to enhance coverage for employees. For example, according to a survey by the Consumer Federation of America and American Council of Life Insurers, 82 percent of workers either have no long-term disability coverage or have coverage they believe is inadequate. Using this example, you can begin the sales process by obtaining an "electronic" census of employees to develop recommendations that are in line with the demographics of the company.

To enhance your chance for success, establish a company contact for the application process. You can partner with this contact when you are trying to solidify a strategy or gain commitment for the specifics of a case. In addition, make sure that the application period is different from the time your clients are completing other applications. Also, install a variety of precommunication systems with the company by establishing, via email and the telephone, two or three contacts prior to group meetings.

Then, schedule a group introduction meeting to last 15 minutes, followed by a second email communication with a link to your carrier's website for needs assessment and policy application or to arrange for face-to-face meetings. Keep in mind, however, that electronic processes should not replace offline procedures for employees who may prefer paper-based methods. Finally, close the loop by following up via the telephone.

During the educational process, you can convince most of your prospects not to use traditional, paper-based methods by encouraging them to use online tools to review their current, personal financial situations. Make sure there are opt-out opportunities for those who prefer to continue using the paper-based process. Those who choose the online path can preview their products and services, and select the benefits they need. Alternatively, traditionalists can receive paper proposals, with little room for self-assessment. They can later request paper materials, including printed application forms, if they are interested.

During the application process, your clients may choose to apply for coverage on the Internet, answering questions and viewing pre-populated, state-specific applications online. They can complete their applications with new, button-click, e-signature capabilities, which require no paper or "wet" (pen) signatures. Information about applications is directly fed into the company's administrative systems. "Clean applications" are auto-issued, and policies are ready for delivery to the client within 24 hours.

Furthermore, electronically driven tracking systems are available to you and benefits administrators to monitor case application progress, maintain momentum and achieve participation levels.

Internet-based alternatives also exist to help you manage your administrative functions. Explore options for "one-touch-and-done" billing and collection services (electronic billing and payment), which are tied to a secure, Web-based interface, and offer access to account information seven days a week. This online-billing method allows administrators to schedule and revise individual (list billed policy) information and review billing and payment history.

What's more, e-billing reduces the likelihood of administrative problems occurring and enables you to spend more time selling and less time troubleshooting. It also allows you to gain access to updated information on all your client accounts.

And while considering e-bill and e-pay capabilities designed for the workplace, consider the fact that according to Eastbridge Consulting Group's *Worksite MarketVision 1998*, the payroll-deduction benefit and the convenience of purchasing products at work remain the top two reasons an employee purchases a voluntary benefit product. Put this finding to the test by selling a supplemental insurance policy via the Internet.

As demonstrated in this crash course on online tools for selling voluntary benefits, you can impact business literally with the touch of a button. Whether you are selling a policy to an individual or via employer-endorsed cases, interchanging traditional with online-selling methods can be a cost-effective and efficient way to enhance your practice without significantly changing your traditional sales practices. Ask your carrier for further direction or search the information super-highway for alternative routes to test-drive available options. Then, it's up to you and your clients to chart a suitable, win-win course to a destination—sales for you and coverage for them.

Hal Sizer, RHU, is a general sales manager for Massachusetts Mutual Life Insurance Co. He has more than 17 years of disability income insurance experience. You can reach him at hsizer@massmutual.com *or at 860-987-2426.*

HEALTH INSURANCE

Here are some points for selling health savings accounts when meeting with prospects:

- Employers can cut premiums by 25 percent to 40 percent, contribute to the employees' HSAs and still save money.

- Small businesses will purchase HSAs because—unlike the old medical savings accounts—employees can make contributions to the accounts.

- Employees will be more judicious when they are seeking medical attention if they write a check to partially cover expenses.

- Employees can roll over the funds left in the HSA at the end of every year.

(Reported by David Connell, editor of Advisor Today*)*

Find the premium dollars.

I do a lot of individual health insurance sales. When I sit down with a family to plan their health insurance coverage, the client invariably wants to know what first-dollar coverage costs.

After showing that, I offer a plan with a $500 or $250 deductible. I also show a higher deductible plan, suggesting that the family self-fund the difference between the deductibles and use the difference in the premium to buy disability income insurance on the main bread-winner in the family. Or if the family needs permanent life insurance, I suggest that the client put the difference into a permanent life insurance contract.

By using time-value of money charts, I show what the money would do for the family if it were invested at different interest rates. Then I take a chart and show what the money would do if it were put into a permanent life insurance policy. I have made numerous sales just by finding premium dollars with this approach.

Carl W. Cox CLU, ChFC, is an advisor with Ky Farm Bureau Insurance in Elizabethtown, Ky. He can be reached at 270-737-7377 or at carl_cox@kyfbins.com.

Sell waiver-of-premium benefits.

When I speak to my self-employed clients about their group health-care contracts, I remind them that even though they may be paying several hundred dollars for family coverage, they still do not have a waiver-of-premium benefit during an extended illness.

"If you are hospitalized or disabled, the premium has to be paid for the health contract to stay in force and keep paying benefits," I point out. "And how will you pay for food, clothing and utilities and meet the mortgage and car payments, as well as take care of all your disability needs?"

Emphasizing the added protection that a policy with a waiver of premium offers usually convinces the client to buy because he realizes how financially devastating an extended illness could be.

Bruce A. Dahms, LUTCF, is an agent in Dixon, Iowa. He can be reached at 563-843-3700 or through baumer@netins.net.

Look what I found!
When you are selling individual health coverage, always show the monthly premiums for various deductible plans. The premium savings between plans of $250, $500, $1,000 and $2,500 deductibles can be $50 to $100 per month.

The "found" money can then be used to purchase additional cash-value life insurance. In a few years, the cash value of the policy will more than cover the higher deductible on the health policy.

Charles C. Avatar, CLU, ChFC, LUTCF, RHU, is with First Financial Group, Mass Mutual, Somerdale, N.J. You may contact him at 609-324-1687 or at charlesavatar@msn.com.

Fan belts not covered!
A large percentage of our health premiums pay for the administration of small claims. Sometimes, the benefit due the insured is as much as it costs to process a claim. We do not buy car insurance to pay for broken fan belts or flat tires. Why, then, do we sell comprehensive major medical to cover small outpatient bills? Why not sell a per-illness, hospital-only plan that offers an outpatient catastrophic illness rider?

Additionally, sell a plan that offers a high hospital deductible and a stop-loss of $10,000. This combination could save your client 40 percent to 50 percent over a traditional plan. This is money that could be used to buy a universal life vehicle that provides a ready reserve for unusually high medical expense years.

James B. Henderson, RHU, is with Group Alternative Inc.
in Metairie, La. You may reach him at 504-712-8955.

MORTGAGES

Help clients get rid of the mortgage millstone.

I tell all my prospects and clients: "Your mortgage is, in reality, a millstone around your neck. We can remove it and give your family a roof over their heads with mortgage insurance."

I add: "Because of your life insurance, if something happens to you, Jane has the house free and clear. If Jane dies, you have the money to pay off the mortgage."

We use adjustable life with a term rider on it for the spouse. At the end of the mortgage, the client can take the cash value in the policy or leave the policy intact and use it for some other life insurance need. Another option is that the client can, at age 65, use the cash value in the policy to buy an annuity. With people living longer, a supplemental annuity may be important to help the client maintain a lifestyle he has become accustomed to.

Stanley Lipman, CLU, is an advisor with AXA Advisors LLC
in Manasquan, N.J. He can be reached at 732-528-6900.

ANNUITIES

Use an acronym to remember annuity benefits when talking to prospects.

 We know we have to focus on the benefits our products provide when talking with our prospects. When recommending annuities, there is a simple acronym I use to remember the main benefits of annuities.

The acronym is SIFT and stands for:

- Safety

- Interest

- Flexibility (access)

- Tax deferral

When focusing on this acronym, be sure you speak in terms of how the prospect or the client will benefit from the annuity.

Greg Ongna is with Farm Bureau Financial Services. Contact him at 515-226-6188.

Remember to buy high, not low, when it comes to annuitization.

We've all heard the adage that we should buy low and sell high. This may be good advice for many investments, but it certainly is not good advice when suggesting a fixed, single-premium immediate annuity or the annuitization of a retirement plan.

Two of the factors that make up the payout rates for annuitization are mortality and interest rates. Both are used in determining the benefits under an annuity plan when a life option is a part of the equation. While mortality doesn't affect a period-certain annuitization, the current interest rates certainly do. Many people are not aware that when they commit to an irrevocable annuity option, they have usually locked in, for the duration of the contract, the payout rates based on the interest-rate environment and the mortality assumptions in effect at the time of that election.

Instead of committing your clients to this decision when rates are low, see if there are alternatives. Consider establishing a systematic withdrawal from their deferred annuity or retirement plan, if available. Some qualified plans may allow the participant to park the money for a period of time. If they have to annuitize or take a series of payments, consider annuitization or receiving payments in a way the funds can roll into an individual retirement account until the interest rate environment is more favorable. Then, if they wish, they can buy a single-premium immediate annuity, or they can annuitize. However, this may not work if the payments are considered part of a series of substantially equal periodic payments of 10 years or more.

For nonqualified funds, some companies now allow for the funds to come out in such a way that you still get the benefit of the exclusion ratio. However, you do not have to commit to a plan that is irrevocable beyond a certain time frame. (This is sometimes referred to as the access period.) In this way, you can get the benefits of the exclusion ratio now, but have the option to commit to a life or a period-certain payout when the interest rates are higher.

Therefore, you must remember to buy high, not low, when it comes to annuitization.

Robert Lee Bateman is a principal in Bateman & Co. in Ogden, Utah. Contact him at 801-475-8121.